fabulous fabric paint

making magic on material

fabulous fabric paint

monique day-wilde & angie franke

METZ PRESS

Acknowledgements

Thanks to our parents, extended families and friends, for getting us
as far as we are;
Michael Day and Michael Franke, John, Michael Tristan, Elizabeth Louise,
Gemma and Joshua (for not complaining too much about their
dinners – or lack thereof!);
Peter Weisswange;
Xoliswa Maureen Yozo, Nondomiso Gloria Qobo;
Suan Landman, Shelagh Johnston, Moira-Lee Purdon, Bernie Millar,
Lindsay Woods, Clara Klitsie and the Calendar Girls;
Wilsia Metz, for taking us on!
And last but not least, our very supportive painters.

The authors and publisher also extend heartfelt thanks to the kind people who
so graciously allowed us into their wonderful homes to take photographs:
Dr Jeanette Bruwer (Springfield), Susan van der Schijff, Lindie Metz, Jeanette
Bruwer (Randrivier B&B) and the Weiswange and Van Niekerk families

Published by Metz Press
1 Cameronians Avenue
Welgemoed, 7530
South Africa

First published in 2005
Copyright © Metz Press 2005
Text copyright © Monique Day-Wilde, Angie Franke
Photographs copyright © Metz Press

All rights reserved. No part of this publication may be reproduced, stored in a retrieval system or transmitted in any form or by any means, electronic, mechanical, photocopying, recording or otherwise, without the prior written permission of the copyright owners.

PUBLISHER AND EDITOR	Wilsia Metz
DESIGN AND LAY-OUT	Alinda Metz
PHOTOGRAPHER	Ivan Naudé
REPRODUCTION	Cape Imaging Bureau, Cape Town
PRINTING AND BINDING	Printed and bound in Singapore by Star Standard
ISBN	1-919992-21-9

Contents

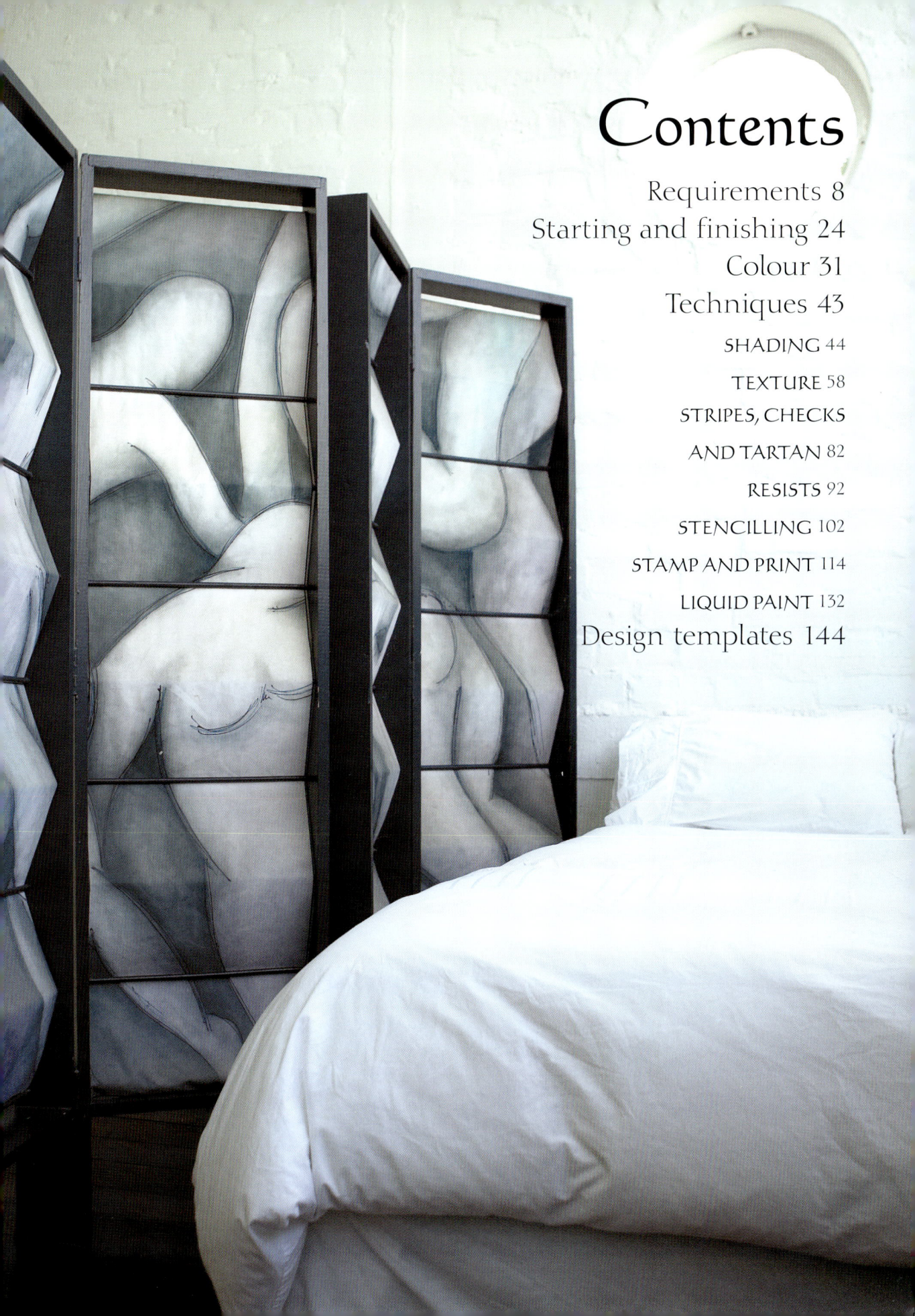

Requirements 8
Starting and finishing 24
Colour 31
Techniques 43
SHADING 44
TEXTURE 58
STRIPES, CHECKS
AND TARTAN 82
RESISTS 92
STENCILLING 102
STAMP AND PRINT 114
LIQUID PAINT 132
Design templates 144

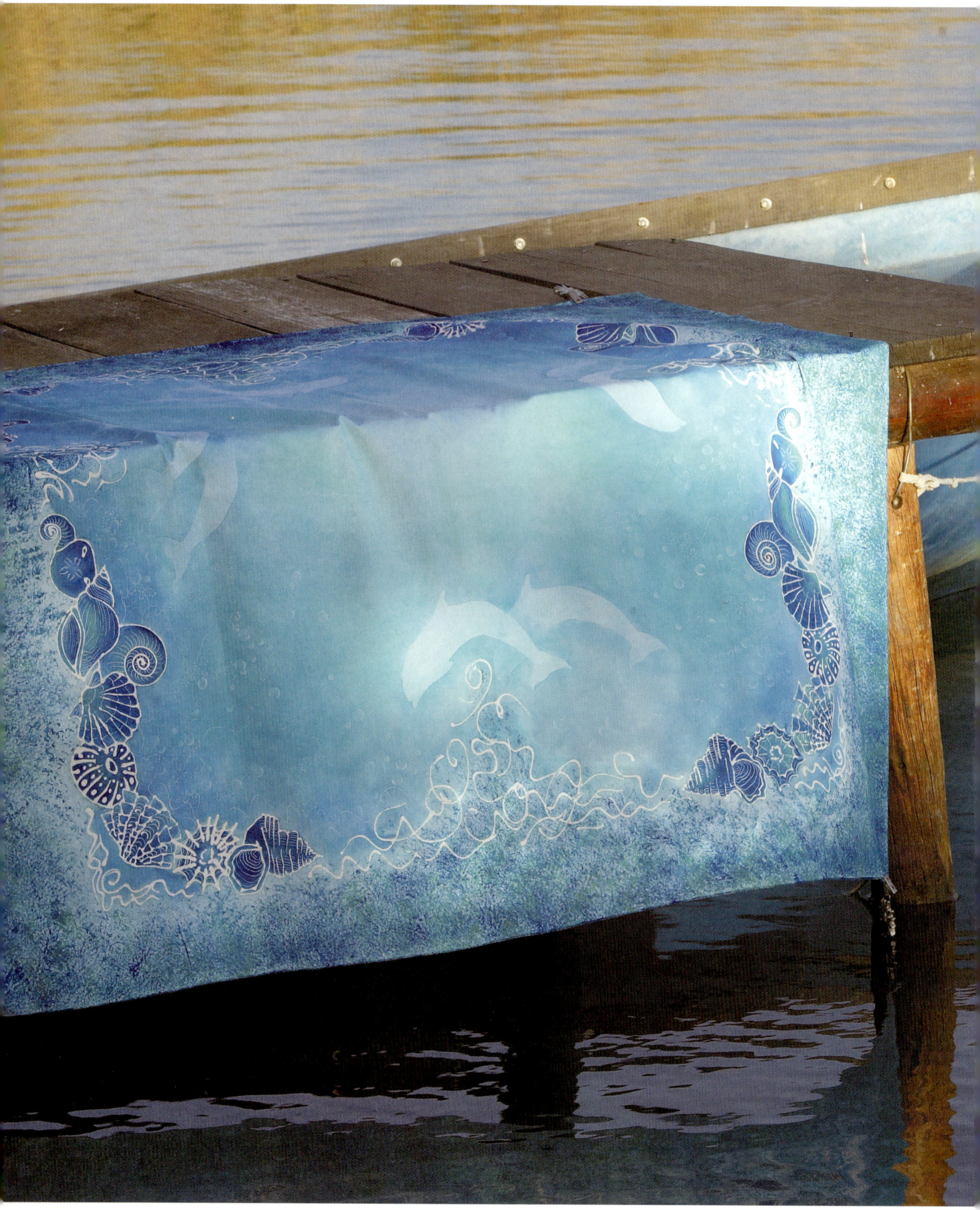

Fabric painting is a forgiving craft where art and fashion come together and you can bring your individual touch to create magic on fabric! There are so many techniques, each with its own style, that we're often left wondering how an item was painted. In this book we explore as many techniques as possible, giving tips along the way.

Fabric painting is for everyone, and not an exclusive art form. We delight in debunking the myth surrounding the magic status of artists. If you have no confidence in your creativity you may surprise yourself on your journey of discovery. It is a great joy to us as teachers to to share our secrets – though we've received more than we've given over the years. For this we thank our very supportive painters.

basics

Requirements

In addition to fabric and paint, you need certain basic tools for fabric painting. Most of these will be used many times over.

A simple piece of cotton painted with the lapis lazuli technique was draped over an old piano stool for an instant revamp.

Fabric

Most paint manufacturers recommend 100% cotton fabric or other natural fibres, as these give the best results. This includes some types of sheeting, denim, bull denim, calico (bleached and unbleached, though watch out for polycotton blends), percale cotton, canvas, lawn, cheesecloth, muslin, and so on. Don't use fabric that is too thin, to begin with, as it can be more difficult to control.

BURN TEST

If you are unsure of the fabric content, do the burn test. This will categorise the fabric, though not give an exact identification. Burn a small sample of your fabric. If it is cotton, flax or silk it will not shrink away from the flame, but ignite on contact. It will burn quickly with an afterglow when finished. The residue will be light and ash-like, light to charcoal grey in colour.

Acrylic, polyester and nylon, though igniting readily, will melt and fuse away from the flame. They will burn rapidly with a flame and are self-extinguishing. An irregular, hard black bead will be left. In the case of yarns composed of two or more fibres, the test will usually give the reaction of the fibre that burns most easily.

SYNTHETICS

Some fabric paints work well on polycotton as well, though expect the painted area to lighten, as the polyester content of the fabric does not absorb the paint and this will then wash out, leaving the fabric looking faded.

A binder medium can be added to fabric paint, which makes ordinary paint completely colourfast on synthetics. This opens up a world of possibilities: we've painted successfully on chiffon, velvet, peach skin, nylon, polyester and acrylics using binder medium with our ordinary fabric paint.

Lycra, Quantec (parachuting), as well as fabric for outdoor use, need special paints. These would be sold under various trade names, so consult your local information directory for a good silk-screen supplier, for instance. You can of course use the PVA based paints to paint fabric but this leaves cloths stiff, without that soft handle fabric should have.

PREPARATION

Always wash the fabric to remove starch or sizing before you use it. This has a marked effect on the colourfastness of the fabric once it is painted. Normal washing powder is fine, but don't use fabric softener as it affects the take-up of paint into the fibres.

Some fabrics are labelled 'prepared for printing' which means that they are pre-shrunk and un-sized and can therefore be used immediately without washing and ironing. Always check with the supplier and if in doubt – wash. Edge first if your item needs a rolled hem on the overlocker. If you are going to sew a normal hem or finish in another way, then paint first otherwise your hem will show as a darker line.

Paint and colour

Paint consists of a colour (pigment), mixed with a binder (base), to make it adhere to a surface. The type of base used to bond the colour is determined by the surface to be coated and the durability required.

Fabric paints are available in many different finishes: transparent, opaque, pearlized (metallic), and fluorescent. Pigment dye is also used as paint. Paints react differently, depending on the weight and nature of the fabric used. Most pearlized, opaque and fluorescent paints sit on the cloth, as opposed to transparent paint and pigment dye, which are absorbed.

The consistency of bought fabric paint should be creamy and free of lumps. Decant paint as required, as containers should be kept closed to prevent paint from drying out. Should mould occur, scoop it off, add a small amount of Savlon or mineral turpentine – ¼ teaspoon per cup – and mix well. Invert your paint container if you will be storing paint for a long time. This excludes air and reduces the possibility of mould. If your paint becomes

Both fabric and technique were used for a variety of textural effects in this selection of cushions.

OPAQUE

Painting with opaque fabric paint is very different from painting with transparent-based paint. Opaques have been especially created to show up on a dark background and can be used to work over already painted items, completely or partially blocking out what is underneath, depending on their density (or degree of opacity). There is a variety of different opaque bases available for different applications.

With pigments added, the complete range of colours can be mixed. Some opaque paints are sold as partially or semi-opaque if they have extender added to them to soften the degree of cover.

Complete or true opaques actually rest on the surface of the cloth and tend to make it feel stiff, if used excessively. But as they block out the colour of the fabric, they are ideal if you are covering darker cloth – or mistakes! They can also be over-dyed successfully (acting as a resist). In this case, heat set the paint *before* dyeing.

Opaque bases

There are two commonly used opaque bases, namely Opaque WHITE Base and Opaque Base. Be very careful when buying them if you mix your own paints from pigments and base. *Much confusion surrounds this point so read labels carefully*.

When mixing with opaque white, you automatically render your colour opaque and pastel – even with loads of pigment added, these colours remain pastel. For instance, red pigment added to white opaque base would always come out pink. But if you mix red pigment with opaque base it will show up red.

thick, add small amounts of warm water, mixing well, until the desired consistency is reached – add a little Savlon or turpentine, as most water is not sterile. Salt can also dilute paint, but may reduce colourfastness, especially in hard-water areas – **beware**!

TRANSPARENT

Transparent paint has a clear emulsion base to which colour (pigment) has been added. The clear emulsion base is also known as extender, transparent base and cut clear. It is water based, which means that it may be diluted with water, and needs to be heat set. As this paint is transparent, layering colours over each other can create wonderful effects. The layer underneath will affect the colour on top, for example if you paint blue on top of yellow, the colour achieved will be green. You can create great shading effects by painting one colour on top of another.

Plain opaque-based paints are tricky to work with as they are semi-transparent while they are still wet and only show their true bright colours when bone dry. They then feel very chalky to the touch and have a matte finish. They can be worked over when dry and shaded with transparent-based paints. This is much easier than trying to shade them while wet as you struggle to see what you are doing. The transparent-based colours dry to a faint sheen changing the harsh chalky look of the dried opaques to a smoother finish.

Hint
White paint is completely different from opaque white base. White paint is transparent base or extender with white pigment added and is used for making strong transparent pastels when mixing it with transparent based colours. Simply adding extender to colours lightens them and doesn't really render them pastel.

Opaque medium
Opaque medium added to ordinary transparent-based paint renders the paint opaque, with the degree of opacity depending on the quantity used. As opaque medium is fairly expensive it is not advisable to use it on big projects. Keep a bottle handy for those small areas that need the addition of a little opaque highlight.

SHEEN
Pearlescent base can be mixed with any bought pigments to create shiny, pearly paints of any colour – useful for highlights and special occasion cloths. This is very expensive and the most cost-effective solution is to buy a range of pearly liners – if you need to, you can unscrew the bottle and apply the paint directly with a brush.

For metallic effects, you can buy gold, copper, silver and bronze paints and liners ready-made. You can also make your own by using pearlescent base with yellow, brown, red and grey pigments to create similar effects.

Embossing powder can be dusted or blown with a puffer (use a liner bottle filled with powder) onto wet paint to create a bright metallic effect such as gold leaf (see page 120).

For glitter effects, either buy ready-made paint-on glitter from your sup-

This organza tea shower was stencilled all over with opaque white. As I knew that the organza would act somewhat like a silkscreen, and that my work surface would also have daisies all over it, I decided to make two cloths for the price of one, you could say. I pinned the organza to a piece of white fabric about the same size (it could have been any colour), and stencilled the daisies where I needed them by applying opaque white with a sponge roller. When I had completed as many as I wanted, I gently removed the organza, which now had daisies stencilled on it – as did the cloth underneath. Leaving both to dry, I now had a tea shower, which I finished with a rolled hem and beads. I also had a 'white on white' cloth for something else!

Friend and fellow fabric painter, Carmel Wolf, painted her own adaptation of a personal favourite: Gustav Klimt's The Kiss. She experimented with transparent, opaque and mostly pearl paints: stamping, outlining, combing, scraping and layering the paints to give a very textured and lively look to this richly coloured and exquisite section. Many different applicators were used – from forks to corks – with real leaves, potato stamps, brushes, liners and sponges for good measure.

plier, or use glitter appliqué glue or make your own. Mix glitter into fabric glue *(not* pressure sensitive glue, but the kind used by appliqué artists). Apply this over your dried, coloured fabric paint to highlight it. The fabric glue dries clear, but will feel a little stiffer than the fabric around it. Don't be tempted to mix the fabric glue and glitter into the paint while wet. This dilutes the glue's efficacy and the glitter will simply wash out. (We've tried it!)

A wide range of glitter liners is available, as well as fine glitter powders and sparkle dust, which can be mixed with all paints or blown onto wet paint or fabric glues. Experiment with these, but remember to follow any special care instructions on the packaging.

PIGMENT DYE/SUN PAINT

These are made up from fabric paint pigment, but instead of having an emulsion base, they are mixed with a liquid fixer which binds them to the fabric. All the same rules for colour mixing and colourfastness apply, but application can differ.

The liquid 'paints' can be sprayed, wet painted and can be useful for paint-on-dye techniques (as for batik work). The advantage here is that they are excellent cold-water dyes, with great intensity of colour and may be diluted to achieve paler results.

They can double as silk paints as well. The liquid paint flows really well on silk. On heavier fabrics, the dye will flow easier if the fabric is dampened first. The degree of flow and intensity of colour will be reduced by the thickness and absorption of the fibre. These paints can be used with fine stencil work if a stencil brush (see page 14), is used. It is also ideal for spraying or spattering through stencils with an atomizer, airbrush or toothbrush. Liquid paints are also marketed under the sun paint labels.

OTHER MEDIUMS

Several other mediums can be used decoratively.

Synthetic colour

Synthetic oranges, purples and greens cannot be mixed from primaries. The paint or pigment is bought as is.

Fluorescents are emulsion-based paints in a limited range of colours, in transparent, opaque and shiny. They need to be heat set.

Anti-bleed or binder medium

These liquids can be added to paints to prevent bleeding or seepage of paint when working on fine weaves, sheer and synthetic fabrics. Follow the manufacturer's instructions carefully. If you add too much, your paint will gel or stiffen and become unusable. Then even trying to dilute the paint with warm water doesn't work! Heat set according to the fabric type.

Kokis

Fabric kokis are available in a limited range of colours. While they may claim to be colourfast, it is always best to work over them with a layer of clear emulsion to seal them, as they tend to fade or change colour with time. Heat set as if painted.

Liners

These are available in a limited range of colour. You can add to the range by simply putting fabric paint into liner bottles yourself (see page 16–17).

Pastels and crayons

These are similar to those used on paper. They are used in the same way and create similar effects and are available at most craft shops. They are nice to use as resists for water-colour effects and great for kids' projects.

Tracing tools

Before paint is applied, most people will want to trace or draw their design onto the fabric. HB and softer (2B and 4B) pencils are fine for some designs, though remember that this will not wash out. Rubbing out with an eraser causes pilling. Charcoal is sometimes used, but can be messy if smudged.

Coloured chalks work well and are easily removed by washing but bear in mind that anything painted over with transparent-based paint or extender is sealed in and will not wash out easily. White and yellow chalks work well on dark fabrics (see page 26). China markers (the kind wrapped in tear-off paper spirals) also draw well on dark fabric. Slivers of dressmaker's chalks are effective when drawing fine lines freehand on dark cloths.

Purple tailor's pens are fine if you paint straight away. They fade quickly, though – especially in humid weather. A blue tailor's pen works quite well as it washes out, either when painting with water-based paint or when the fabric is washed. Don't use it on silk or similar fabric, as it tends to stain. If in doubt, try on a small swatch first. *The fabric must be washed at some stage, if this blue pen is used, as it eats away at the fibres over time.*

Various dressmaking pencils work as well as ordinary lead pencils and the colours can be more easily absorbed into a design. But beware of coloured pencils and overhead projector markers or kokis as they dissolve in wet paint and bleed, sealing into the paint and thus ruining a design.

I used several techniques in this table cloth. The design was outlined in starch paste. When the starch was dry I sponged with a light green, over which darker colours were painted with a brush, so that the brushstrokes would show. Some leaf details were scratched into the wet paint with the back of a brush. A small lizard stamp was used to add a quirky stamped-off detail. Before the starch resist was removed, I applied yellow and mauve liquid paint to the back of the cloth, colouring the starch lines. This technique is better suited to darker cloths, as the liquid paint can be patchy when dry and will show through on lighter cloths. The starch was removed when the cloth was completely dry.

Tools for colour

Just about anything can be used to apply paint to fabric – each creating its own effect. You can be as adventurous as you want to be, but never apply the paint too thickly. This will result in a plastic feel when the paint is dry, which is not pleasant, particularly if the painted item is a garment.

Here are a few examples of suitable applicators:

BRUSHES

You can use any type or size of brush for fabric painting, depending on the technique used.

Cheap china brushes used for oil painting are best. They offer good value for money and, if looked after, will last a long time (years!). They come coated with a special starch to keep bristles stiff. Work the bristles between your fingers to soften them before use. The square tipped brushes are the most versatile, though the rounded ones are certainly useful. A good selection of sizes is useful; get # 1, 4, 8 and 12 to begin with. The higher the number the larger the brush.

Watercolour brushes work really well for finer painting and liquid paint effects. It is not necessary to buy the really expensive sable or hog's hair brushes – the nylon ones work well.

Ordinary wall and roof painting brushes do a great job on large items. It's very liberating to slosh large quantities of paint over a huge cloth! They work well as stipplers for textured backgrounds or floggers for special effects. Stencil brushes are round with short, stiff bristles for dabbing (pouncing), and hake brushes are ultra finefor softening and blurring.

Care of brushes

Always clean your brushes well. Dab

them into washing up liquid (a Sunlight soap bar is even better, as it contains no detergent and the fat content bonds with the paint and removes it completely), wash thoroughly, rinse and wipe. Squeeze the bristles flat with your fingers and allow to dry – this helps retain their shape. The best way to dry brushes is to hang them from the handles, though drying flat will do. Never leave brushes standing on their bristles for long periods, either in water or in a container to dry. This damages the bristles and the brush won't work properly with bent bristles.

If a brush has lost its shape, wash and coat with washing up liquid, flatten and leave to dry. Rinse before use. Coat brushes with Vaseline if they are going to be stored for a long time.

Brushes with long bristles that splay in all directions can be shaped by 'painting' a piece of medium grit sandpaper, backwards and forwards in all directions. This may take a while but is worth the effort.

Dry-brush a few ceramic items first with new brushes to wear them down and shape them. A quicker, more drastic way to thin a stiff, chunky-bristled brush is to stand the bristles in undiluted bleach for a minute or two and then neutralise it immediately in vinegar. Rinse the brush well and you will find it magically thinned and shaped! This only works for natural bristles, not for nylon. Take care when you use this method – you don't want to waste your brush away entirely.

SPONGES

A variety of sponges can be used. Each type will give its own, very different effect, depending on the texture of the sponge.

Large bath sponges are great to fill in backgrounds and to create cloudy effects. Sponge applicators on sticks are available from craft shops, and are useful for adding details. Shaped sponges (buy or cut yourself) are great for stamping. High density sponge (available from speciality shops or upholsterers) works well, as does packing sponge.

Sponge rollers of different widths are often used for borders, tartans and stripes. They are not that economical, though, as they absorb a lot of paint, which is ultimately wasted. Rather use short-pile rollers available from paint or hardware shops. Mini sponge rollers are available from stamping suppliers. Rollers with different cut designs are also fun to use.

This design was drawn in black permanent marker and repeated around the cloth. Using various shades of yellow, orange and green, the fruit and leaves were painted in quite roughly, highlighted and shaded by using dry brush and darker shades. Small stencils of the blossoms were placed in position to block out the area while painting the background. A pale blue was applied with a sponge and then shaded over with a darker blue. The cloth is darker in the middle and the edges and lighter towards the fruit. Once the stencils were removed, the white blossoms only needed a small yellow dab in the centre to make them come alive.

Sea sponges are useful for different textural effects but are expensive, and there are certainly other alternatives. For instance, you could pick holes in a bath sponge (or give it to your dog to chew – mine did a good job!) and use that instead.

Wash and rinse sponges thoroughly after use or the colour from your previous project could make an unwelcome reappearance!

SQUEEGEES

Using a squeegee is a quick way to fill a cloth with solid colour, and great for backgrounds or borders. You can use the screen-printing variety (which is expensive), or simple window-cleaning squeegees. Dip the squeegee into paint or blob paint in different areas on the cloth. Pull the squeegee firmly over the cloth at a slight angle. You will have an even spread of mixed or plain colours. Repeat over the area required. You can work over this with opaque or darker colours.

OTHER IDEAS

Credit type cards such as used phone cards (not your current visa!), tile glue applicators and paint scrapers are great paint applicators, as is a hard piece of cardboard. These also give interesting textural effects.

Scrunched up plastic bags, bubble wrap, or other similar items will give a textural effect when applied lightly.

Items such as a cork, hard vegetables, erasers, absorbent kitchen cloths, and so on work well as stamps. This list can go on and on, but we do give further ideas throughout the techniques discussed.

LINERS

There are a number of ways to create lines.

Fine scrapers

The simplest tools to create lines in paint are items which can be scraped over wet paint – the back of your brush, a bamboo skewer, a knitting needle, an empty ball point pen, a fork, a twig and even long fingernails!

Feathers are wonderful for dragging lines when creating marbling and lapis-lazuli effects.

Liner bottles

Most fabric-paint manufacturers have a range of colours available in liner bottles. There is nothing magic in liner paint – it is the same as the ordinary

The butterflies were photocopies transferred with thinners (see page 123). They were painted in with transparent paint. The pearl and glitter liner used as a finishing touch made all the difference. Liners were also used for the dots and spirals in the background.

paint we use, so it is cheaper to fill your own liner bottles. If the paint is thick, such as opaque paint, it may need to be thinned with a few drops of warm water or extender.

Always start with paint in a container, adding a little water as you go, to obtain a smooth result. It is important that the paint is not lumpy, as this will block the liner nozzle.

Liner bottles come in many varieties, but the small, soft ones, which fit comfortably into your palm, allow you to squeeze them more easily, ensuring even application of the liner. Most liner bottles have plastic nozzles, though craft shops also sell metal ones which give a finer line. If you are battling to find a metal nozzle you can use the metal tip of a clutch pencil. Stick it on with masking tape, or screw it onto an existing nozzle top.

It is important to keep the nozzle clean, ideally every time you use it. However, if you're like us, you just leave it and the paint dries inside the tip, blocking the flow and adding to your frustration levels! Don't throw the bottle across the room – the nozzle is relatively easy to clean. Unscrew it, flush with warm water and brush with a paintbrush. If there is still paint stuck in the tip, insert a thin needle from the inside out, thus releasing the blockage. At the same time check the quality of the contents of your liner bottle. If you've left it for too long you may need to start cleaning and filling from scratch!

Perm-lotion bottles make good liner bottles. Another idea for a liner is to put watered down paint into an underarm deodorant roller-bottle. While a little thick, this can create quite interesting effects.

Share a secret (or two)

- To fill a liner bottle: insert a small funnel into the bottle and fill with paint. Lift funnel slightly and create a vacuum in the bottle by squeezing it flat. Drop funnel back to seal bottle opening and release squeeze. The paint will be magically suctioned into the bottle.
- Syringes can be useful for filling liner bottles and for carefully measuring small amounts of paint while mixing colours.
- Don't cut the top off a new liner to make the opening; the hole will be too large. Stick a pin into the top.
- Smudged your liner? Try working it into your design with a brush and leave to dry. Add a contrasting liner on top of this. If smudged liner is metallic, leave to dry for three days and hand wash. The metallic paint will wash out.

OPPOSITE PAGE *It was one of those days when I really didn't know what I wanted to paint – just that it should be a large cloth and that I wanted to use greys and oranges (although orange isn't my favourite colour). I started by covering the central area with a pale grey and slopping on some darker grey and a little orange. Then I worked it in with a brush, creating a clouded patchy texture. I added triangles and squares in orange, picking up a number of shades at once, again creating a patchy effect. I didn't worry about hard edges to the shapes. I wet the outside border with pale grey and brushed on greys and oranges, though darker this time than in the centre. I added black and navy liner which I flattened with my finger, adding to the texture. The result of my playing and not worrying about keeping in the lines is an unusual and interesting cloth. I dare you!*

Acrylic liners

There are also acrylic liners available in metal tubes from art shops. These are expensive and not as easy to use as the soft liner bottles.

Pens

Some folk use the waterproof liner-pens, but they can blob and bleed. We suggest you stick to the fabric pens which look and feel like kokis. They are available at most craft or art shops. Unless painted over in the normal painting process, it is a good idea to paint over drawn lines with clear extender, and to fix the colour well, as these pens inevitably fade.

Use permanent gel-markers for very fine lines. Milky pens work wonderfully on dark and black fabrics and while they are washable, seal over them with extender to render them completely permanent. Quilters use them for fine work.

Special blank fibre-tip pens are available at cake decorating shops for use with food colouring. Buy a set and fill with liquid fabric-dyes to make your own special, coloured markers.

SHARE A SECRET

Don't discard the blue and purple vanishing pens when dry. Open them and take out the soft fibre filament inside the tube and the compressed fibre writing point or nib. Soak these in water with a little white vinegar. Rinse and squeeze them clean under running water until the colour has disappeared. Allow to dry and stand in a strong pigment-dye solution of whatever colour you require, reassemble and use: your own free permanent fabric marker!

RIGHT *This cushion, stencilled in shades of grey was really simple to do. By cutting stencils of squares and using masking tape for the large rectangle, it was finished in no time. The finishing touches of organza, beads and faux fur complete the look of a boudoir cushion.*

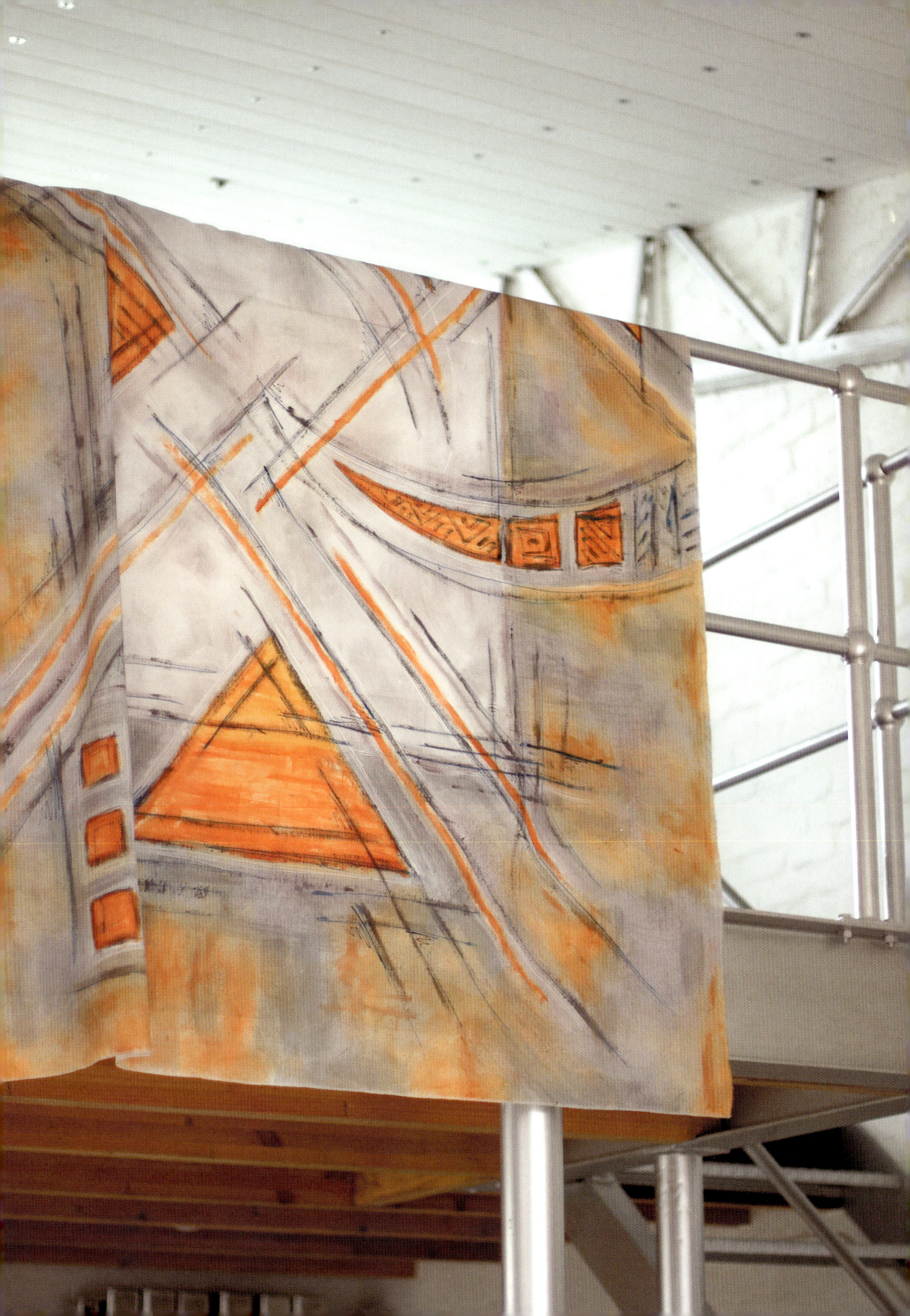

Working surface

A properly prepared working surface is quite important and will depend on the size of the article to be painted. There are a number of options.

Plastic on a table or tray can be very messy and the fabric has a tendency to move around.

For very big cloths, a large old blanket can be useful, provided it is not textured. Instead of moving the cloth, with a good chance of it being smudged, move the blanket around with the cloth on top.

Stretching your fabric in some way so that it is smooth and free of wrinkles makes painting easier. Use a tapestry or canvas frame. You can also stretch it across a piece of plywood and staple, or use masking tape, along the edges. Stretch the fabric as you go. Fabric can be pinned to thick Styrofoam sheeting though these boards are too flimsy for repeated use.

If only these T-shirts could tell their story! Hand me downs are great for practising dyeing and bleaching techniques. Our children had great fun zooting up their old shirts. The orange and navy shirts were spiralled and then sprayed. A rectangle was masked with torn tape, on the green shirt, bleach was sprayed into the rectangle and green paw prints stamped in the space. The small blue shirt was scrunched up and sprayed several times to create the marbled effect. The light pink sunburst on the magenta T-shirt was done with rubber bands and bleach – tie dye in reverse!

STICKY BOARD

We find that by far the most practical, is a 'sticky board' which is portable and very easy to make using pressure sensitive adhesive. Pressure sensitive adhesive table-tack is the same stuff that screen printers use on their printing tables. It is sold as stencil glue an is great for making a working surface or the backs of stencils tacky. When the fabric is spread flat on a sticky board, it forms a lovely smooth, hard surface on which to work – and it won't 'walk' across the table! It is great for smaller items such as cushion covers, placemats, and so on. For T-shirts, cut A3 size boards or X-rays to fit between the front and the back of the shirt.

SHARE A SECRET

To clean an old X-ray, pour a little bleach to cover the X-ray plate. We have found only very strong bleach to be successful. Leave for a minute and scrub off with a dishwashing brush – this keeps your fingers bleach free! Repeat on the reverse side – X-rays are printed on both sides. Rinse very well with clean water until the plate no longer feels slimy. It will now be clear blue and can be used for many applications (see stencilling, page 102). Wear old clothes when you do this!

Making a sticky board

Cover a piece of smooth hardboard, perspex or X-ray with a layer of table tack – about 4 teaspoons to a 50 x 50 cm square. Use a damp cloth, sponge, paintbrush or piece of cardboard to spread the glue onto the surface. Apply it evenly and thinly – lumps and streaks will stop the glue drying uniformly, and could ruin the back of your fabric. It's a good idea to wear a surgical glove or plastic bag on your hand, which can be thrown away after use. The glue is water soluble until dry, after which it needs to be dissolved with meths, spirits or alcohol. Wash and rinse the applicator well after use. Do not wash anything else in the same water.

Leave the board to dry before using – about 15 to 30 minutes. The board should look clear and feel tacky to the touch. Don't try to speed up the drying process with a hairdryer – especially if the board surface is shiny and non-absorbent. The heat of the hairdryer cooks the glue and it comes off the board in gooey lumps. If you have been unable to avoid lumps and streaks, take a piece of scrap cloth with a smooth (*not* fuzzy) finish, and lay this down onto the tacky surface, smoothing down well. Lift the scrap before laying down your project piece.

The same instructions apply to rendering the back of stencils sticky. Again, do not be tempted to dry the glue with a hairdryer (see stencilling, page 102).

Using a sticky board

When you paint on a sticky board, always lift your fabric before it dries, as the paint could form a bond with the glue. If it dries on the board, the painted fabric will be difficult to remove and may even pull up some of the board surface. This does wash off the back of your fabric, but ruins your painting board.

After completing your painting and lifting the fabric, wipe your board until all traces of paint have been removed. Never put paper on a sticky board. Paper *sticks* to the surface and pulls up in shreds, which, of course, ruins the design and means washing the board …!

The backgrounds for these cushions were colour washed in different colours, allowed to dry and stencilled in the same colour as the background to add extra detail. The lavender, daisies, lace flowers and dandelions were painted in afterwards. The flowers on the bought blue gingham cloth were shaded with transparent and opaque white.

ABOVE LEFT *These leafy cloths were painted by Sue Vagionakis in different colour combinations. A number of techniques were used. The border was first traced and painted in using variations of the same colour. The stripes on either side of the large leaves were made using a sponge roller, and finally, the centre was shadow painted, again using leaf shapes, similar to those on the border.*

ABOVE RIGHT *These cloths have all been painted entirely with transparent paint, making use of dry brushing to create the highlights – no opaque white to harden the effect.*

Keep your board as clean as possible. This can be done by sticking some plastic (plain, unprinted shopping bags cut open), onto the surface when the sticky board is not in use. If fluff or loose threads do get onto the surface, wipe with a damp cloth – don't scrub, as the glue could be removed. The first gluing acts as a primer and will last for about three to four painting sessions. Once the board has been re-glued it will remain sticky much longer.

SHARE A SECRET (OR TWO)

- Spilt glue on your new rug? (We had a whole bucket of glue upended on ours!) Flush immediately with clean water and continue until milkiness disappears – it really works!
- Got wet glue on the back of your fabric? Let it dry and rub it off, or use the sticky side of masking tape to lift off spots of dried glue. The glue on masking tape acts similarly to Prestik. Placing a few layers of unprinted newsprint or kitchen towel over the area, and ironing with a hot iron also helps. You can also heat set the cloth and then dissolve the glue carefully with a meths-soaked rag. Meths may affect the paint colour, so work carefully. The best is to avoid all the schlep by doing it properly the first time! Take heed all ye in a hurry!
- For easy removal of old dried paint, a bar of green kitchen soap, foamed and rubbed over the board and left for a few minutes magically softens the paint residue which can be wiped off with a damp cloth. Rinse the board well, leave to dry and the tackiness will return.

MASKING TAPE

Masking tape is available in different widths. It is great for masking borders, checks and stripes. The wider tape can be torn lengthwise to create ragged edges on your work. Bear in mind that masking tape stretches and if stretched while you are pulling it off the roll, may warp or pucker the surface of the fabric. It also has a tendency to curve over long distances, so use good quality tape.

Don't use sticky tape for masking, as it is too smooth and buckles when wet. Wide packaging tape (available in brown or clear) is water resistant and can be used fairly successfully provided you remove it immediately after painting. If not, it bonds with the fabric and leaves a messy, sticky residue.

TAPE MEASURE & RULER

While the measuring aspect speaks for itself, a variety of different width rulers or even a flat stick is really useful for measuring sideways. Place the ruler or stick along the edge of your fabric and stick the masking tape parallel to the ruler, doing this right around the edge of the fabric, so creating a border without measuring out centimetres.

A heavy metal ruler is also great as a guide when painting straight lines or borders. Lay it on the cloth and work the brush, roller, or credit card alongside or against it as you paint. Be careful to wipe the edges clean after lifting and before re-laying it, otherwise you may transfer a line of paint.

SHARE A SECRET (OR TWO)
- Use a piece of cardboard or paper as a guide to measure a border from the outside of the cloth. Make sure your fabric has been cut straight to begin with and use the piece of cardboard in the same direction throughout the measuring process.
- A tape measure with a hole at the end is great for drawing circles.

PRACTICAL GUIDELINES

Some practical guidelines to bear in mind for all the projects:
- Wear protective clothing.
- Practise any new technique first on a fabric off-cut from your previous project.
- Test all new colours by painting swatches – paint lightens when dry.
- Do not leave motifs or backgrounds half done. Joins will show up darker at a later stage.
- For all these projects, the fabric needs to be heat-set when the paint is properly dry.

The cloth hosting this Cape clawless otters was a warm russet colour so I only needed opaque white and transparent brown paints and a liner to brush in the picture. The frame was painted with opaque white fabric paint rubbed over with the same transparent brown. The cloth for the leafy bedcover, a perfect match for the picture, was first sponged in very pale rust, with deeper shades of rust and metallic copper added around the leaves with a brush, while the pale shade was still wet. Blue and rust liner was added in a patchy way around the leaves for definition, and smudged with my finger to enhance the effect. Finally gold was added here and there on the background for extra texture.

Starting and finishing

Finishing your project properly is as important as preparing the fabric for painting and getting your design right.

Design

Design has many elements: colour, pattern, texture, shape and your subjective feelings towards all of these.

How do you decide on a design? Start by asking a multitude of questions: What is the fabric for? How large should it be? If it's a table cloth, should the motifs all 'sit' on or off the table? Should there be a border? If so, what type? And so on. Once you make a start you'll be surprised how everything falls into place.

Even a simple grid made up with leftover starch and painted with leftover colours can make an effective design.

BALANCE

Keep a balance in your design in terms of shape and colour. This doesn't mean that whatever you do should be symmetrical – far from it. The work should have a flow and be easy on the eye, with all elements working together. I have a favourite saying: as long as your work is evenly uneven you're doing fine!

INSPIRATION AND IDEAS

There are many places to explore possibilities – keeping your own design file is a good start. Add to our collection of designs by keeping your own file of articles on fabric painting, and others that catch your eye. Add designs from wrapping papers, magazines, cards, rubber stamps (enlarged on a photo copier) and children's picture storybooks. Raid the juvenile section of your local library.

You'll find wonderful ideas for colours and designs by looking at artwork with interested, analytical and critical eyes. Why did they use those colours? How did they create the effects? Write down interesting colour combinations. Keep snippets of beautiful dress and upholstery fabrics. Look at people in the street, and what they are wearing. What catches your eye and why do you like or dislike it? This can be a lesson in what to avoid!

Look at travel brochures for landscape colours from muted to vibrant. Keep postcards of interesting architectural features to use as design details. Books on botany, astronomy, graphics, animals and so on are great sources of inspiration. Keep seed packets with flower pictures, enlarge colour photos of flowers, and then trace them for accurate designs. Look 'into' the pictures that you see – sometimes the details are far more interesting than the whole, and make for wonderful designs of their own. In short, open your eyes to the wonder of colour and design around you.

Explore and have **fun** painting. It's very therapeutic.

COPYRIGHT

Having given all this advice about looking around you and using what you see, we must stress that using other people's work as inspiration and a springboard for your own ideas is fine. Copying directly is not, unless permission is given. Most printed matter will have a copyright logo ©, which prohibits copying without permission from the copyright holder. Craft books, like this one, will usually have a note saying that it is fine to copy the designs for personal use, but not to reproduce them for commercial gain.

Inspired by Hunderdtwasser, this painting is deceptively simple. It hides a number of images within the shading, including a nude. I've used a lot of scratching and stamping off to add to the texture of the different areas.

Bernie Millar chose The Black Madonna *of Czestochowa to copy, in honour of her late Polish father. The original is thought to have been painted in the 4th century AD. This copy was painted on cotton drill with transparent earth tones to simulate the aged look of an Icon. Fine brushes were used to detail the Madonna's veil with gold paint and fine lines scratched in with a skewer while gold liner was added for richness. The brown wooden frame was washed with gold paint and beads attached and textured fabric sponged to pick up the accents of the portrait. The rough texture of the stunning old door makes the perfect backdrop.*

TRACING

Once you've got a design worked out, you need to transfer it to your fabric. Draw patterns in black or dark outlines on paper and slip underneath your fabric. Most fine to medium-weight, light-coloured fabrics are easy to trace onto. If the fabric is too dense to see through, use a light box or a window (with the light coming from behind) or a light under a glass coffee-table.

To transfer a design to dark or denser fabrics, rub chalk on the back of the design to make a kind of 'carbon paper'. Draw on the design lines with an empty ball point pen or soft pencil pressing fairly hard to ensure the design is transferred onto the fabric (see page 18 for details of pens). If there is a lot of chalk dust on the cloth surface once you've lifted the paper, simply dust it off with a soft cloth. You won't remove your chalk lines if you pressed hard enough, but don't press so hard that you tear through the paper.

REPEATING

A design or motif may be repeated many times across a cloth, either at random or according to a grid system. Grids can become quite complex and confusing. We have included some simpler examples (see page 145).

To trace a repeat design onto a tablecloth, simply iron in creases first, as a guide. For example, if the repeat size is 40 x 40 cm, the creases must make a grid of 40 x 40 cm squares.

ENLARGING

This can be done with a photocopier or manually. If you use a photocopier to enlarge a small design to cushion cover size, for example, you can do it in sections and join the sections to make up the size, or take it to a plan copier for a single enlargement. We included the percentage enlargement or reduction required to get to the most popular sizes (see table on page 160). For example, if your design is A2 size, you need a copy of 142% to get to A3. If your design is A5, you need an 803% enlargement to get to A0.

Doing it manually

If you wish to develop your drawing skills, enlarge your picture by hand:

- Draw a grid across the smaller design.
- On a separate larger sheet of paper, draw the frame of the required size.

- Draw a grid of equal proportion to the small grid in this frame. So if you have six squares up and six across on your small design you will need the same number on the larger sheet of paper.
- Draw the design onto the larger paper matching up squares with the smaller design.

Photocopying is much easier!

SHAPES

Squares and rectangles are easy to draw, as are circles. We will also show you an easy way to draw an oval:

How to draw an oval

An oval can be drawn with the help of two pushpins, some string and a pencil (see page 145). The size and form of the oval depends on the length of the string and the distance between the pins. The string must be longer than the distance between the two pins. Tie the string to both pins; hook the pencil into the string pulling it taut and let it draw its own oval around the pins!

How to cut a circle

Fold your fabric into quarters. Attach the end of a measuring tape to the **folded** corner. This can be done by pinning or by knocking a large pin or small nail through the hole at the end of the tape, and into the work surface. (Don't do this on your dining room table!) Hold the other end of the tape and make a mark on the fabric, *half* the diameter you need. Continue these marks, making an arc. Cut along this line (see page 145).

DETAIL

Paying attention to detail on your finished work makes all the difference. Adding just a little more dark shading, texture or embellishments to your finished article can take it from the mundane to a real work of art. But sometimes less is more – an overworked, cluttered painting is disturbing.

We couldn't find tassels to match the colours in this lapis lazuli cushion cover so we made our own using gold lamé sewing thread and matching crochet cotton. We were thrilled with the result as the tassels really finished the cushion cover beautifully. Tassels are as easy to make as pompons and most decorating books have simple instructions.

Finishing

When fabric has been hand-painted, it must always be heat set before being turned into a functional item. You may also want to protect the fabric.

HEAT SETTING

This process is also known as fixing or curing. This can be done in a number of ways, but regardless of the method you use, try to leave your painting to dry for at least three days before curing, and always read the manufacturer's instructions, regarding the use of their paint. Choose one of the following methods:

- Iron on the wrong side with the iron set on the correct setting for the fabric. Each section to be heat set should be ironed for at least three minutes. This is impractical for large items, as it would take ages.
- Heat set with an industrial iron or take your cloth to someone who offers this service.
- The press-type iron is ideal for heat setting. Set the iron at the appropriate setting for the fabric.
- The painted fabric can be tumble dried in an industrial dryer (at a laundry) on the hot setting for at least 30 to 45 minutes, *never* with other wet washing, as smudging can occur. We don't recommend the use of home dryers.
- Bake in your oven uncovered. Preheat the oven to 160 °C. When the oven has reached this temperature, switch it off. Place your pre-folded cloth into a clean oven pan and place into the (clean!) oven. Leave overnight. Take out and iron. Bear in mind that the oven loses heat when switched off, so this method is not suitable for large cloths as the heat will not penetrate.
- Bake in your oven covered in foil. **We prefer this method.** Preheat the oven to 180 °C. Fold your fabric and place it into a double layer of thick foil, shiny side in. Make sure the foil is properly sealed. Place this parcel in the oven for 3 to 5 minutes. Remove, undo, refold the fabric and place back into the foil. Repeat this process a number of times, depending on the size of the cloth. Make sure that the cloth has been thoroughly heated through. Do not answer the phone or play with the kids while you're doing this! Use a timer and take care – you can burn your cloth if you don't. Don't be put off by the strong chemical smell when you open the foil. This normal chemical reaction is your reassurance that the heat setting is working. This method may seem like a lot of fiddling but you are making quite sure that the fabric is well heated through, so nothing will wash out. We wash our heat-set fabric in the washing machine on a cold wash with great success.
- The **best** method of all is to ask a screen-printer to cure your pile fabric in the heat tunnel. Expect to be charged for this service as it takes time and effort. Negotiate a price beforehand.

WASHING

Once your fabric has been heat set, you can wash it on a cold wash in your washing machine. If you are hesitant, wash by hand with a mild detergent. If it feels slimy, the paint is dissolving. Do not rub or scrub the fabric. Rinse carefully, dry flat and waterproof your article to preserve it, as discussed below. If you have used a blue tailor's pen, it is advisable to wash the fabric even if you are going to frame your painting and no blue is showing. The tailor's pen contains chemicals which will cause the fabric to perish if it is not washed out. Although it only happens over time, it is disastrous nonetheless.

SHARE A SECRET
Fabric softener is a no-no on hand-painted fabrics as it can dissolve fabric paint. And be warned – rinsing painted items in salt water (which is recommended for some dyed articles) can dissolve some fabric paint colours such as black. This was discovered at great cost by one of our painters!

PROTECTING THE FABRIC
Various mediums are applied to painted fabric to protect it to a degree.

Fluorocarbon treatment
The best-known treatment is a fluorocarbon treatment, commonly known as scotch guarding (or other trade names). This can be done professionally, usually by dye houses – check your local directory. The medium penetrates the cloth and is undetectable. Although it is expensive, especially on larger surfaces, you can buy this in spray cans and do it yourself.

Binder coating
This medium is available from any good silk-screen supplier and is applied with a squeegee. The binder coating lies on the surface. For painters who supply hand-painted cloths to restaurants, for example, it is more cost effective to have this done in bulk commercially.

PVC
This coating is laminated on and lies on the surface, rendering it wipe-cleanable. The lamination has to be done professionally.

Other options
More accessible options include polyurethane varnish and water-based floor sealer, both of which work well sponged or painted on to the surface. This leaves the item stiff. Canvas suppliers and tentmakers use a waterproofing agent which is reasonably priced, but will need a few coatings to become wipe-cleanable. It leaves the cloth feeling soft and flexible. The strong odour wears off with time.

If the painted item is to be used as clothing, for example an apron, make sure the fabric still has a pleasant feel – or handle – after sealing. One of our painters sealed her apron so well with undiluted wood-glue, it had to be used as a kitchen wall-decoration!

This cheerful fruity apron is the nearest I get to colouring in. Large simple fruit shapes were brushed in with flat, bright colours which were then shaded while wet to give depth and interest to this fruit salad. Fabric-painted items that will be used and washed often should be given suitable surface treatment.

Two stamps were used as the main motifs for this throw and cushions, on a background dragged with magenta, purple and blue. The paisley pattern was stamped off while the paint was wet, with the scroll pattern stamped on once the paint was dry. Note how the colour of the print changes with the background. Lots of liner detail in different colours was added to the stamped off paisley pattern. I had great fun adding all the ribbon, feather and bead embellishments – all we're short of is a few bells and whistles!

More rigid items, such as garden umbrellas, placemats or wall plaques, can be sealed to a fairly stiff finish. Ordinary white wood-glue dries as a stiff sealer, but can be diluted for a slightly softer effect. Other fabric stiffening mediums can also be used to waterproof items that will stay rigid and don't need a soft fabric feel or finish.

Some companies specialising in waterproofing and sealing will take on smaller items at a price. Remember to negotiate this with them before you hand in your work or you could be in for a shock!

Check with your local supplier what is available and don't be afraid to experiment with small quantities on scrap cloths or reject paintings.

SEWING TIPS

This is not a book on sewing, but most of the items you make will require more work after you've painted the cloth. We have found these guidelines useful:

- When making clothing items, trace the clothing pattern pieces onto the fabric before painting the fabric.
- When painting stripes or lines, remember to line them up correctly so that they will correspond on the finished design when sewn.
- Generally cloths are straight-hemmed after painting. Painting over a lumpy hem will result in a darker line. The exception to this is an item with a rolled hem – first overlock and then paint.
- It is advisable to waterproof a finished item although this depends on the method used: for example, waterproof a tablecloth before it is sewn.

Average sizes

These sizes exclude seam allowances and turnover flaps and are in centimetres unless otherwise stated.

- Placemats 30 x 40; 35 x 45
- Cushion covers 40 – 50 square
- Square and rectangular tablecloths 90 – 100 square; 120 x 180; 140 x 220; 150 x 220; 180 x 240; 180 x 270
- Round tablecloths 100; 120; 150; 180; 220; 240
- Pillowcases 45 x 70; 70 x 70; 80 x 80
- Duvet covers
    o   single 130 x 200
    o   three-quarter 150 x 200
    o   double 200 x 200
    o   queen 230 x 200
    o   king 230 x 230

Colour

While a good design is important to the outcome of your project, more than half the battle is won if your colour combination works well. A good design can be ruined with a poor combination and a mediocre design enhanced with good colours.

Inspiration

Every time you visit a paint shop, take a few free sample paint swatches to add to your colour library. Put these samples together, arranged in 'rainbow fans' for inspiration for all your projects. A collage or storyboard can be assembled using a mixture of elements for its own sake and as a catalyst for fresh ideas. Use the paint samples, fabric swatches, your own mixed colour experiments, photos, magazine pictures and other found objects from beads and stickers to interesting bits of stone. We've included an example here (see photograph on the right).

Combinations

Once you have mixed and painted the colours for your own colour wheel, you can use it as a guide for choosing colour combinations. Colours that lie next to each other on the wheel are in harmony with each other. Those that lie opposite are complementary or accent colours. When deciding on a colour combination, it is always safe to work with triangular patterns, for example two in harmony spiked with one accent.

Lighter and darker tones of the same colour live in harmony with each other and are comfortable on the eye. More exciting, though, are combinations that make use of a pair of complementary colours such as blue and orange, or green and red.

The warm colours are the magenta, red, orange, yellow half of the colour wheel, while blue, green, purple, and violet are cool colours. Cool colours are calming and recede, while warmer colours are inviting and exciting.

Colour theory

In our attempts to learn about colour we were first led to how the colour wheel works, and in the process developed our own wheel which is specifically for fabric paint. This step-by-step process of mixing and painting your own colour wheel is one of the best ways for you to learn and gain confidence in using paint and colour. Not only is it helpful in being able to add so many possibilities to your palette, but it saves much time and frustration in sourcing the exact tint or shade you may need to complete a project.

COLOUR WHEEL

The beauty of the wheel in this book (known as Angie's wheel) is the simple way in which it shows the hierarchical relationship of the 12 basic colours, including their tints, shades, earth tones and brown. If you follow the instructions carefully (see page 34) you will be able to paint your own wheel which will be specific to you. Keep it as your most useful colour reference tool.

All the colours on this wheel are mixed from the three primary colours and black and white. The primary colours used for fabric painting are: primrose (yellow), cyan (blue) and magenta (bright, dark pink). These are identical to the primaries used in the printing industry – from big photographic printers to the little inkjet printer linked to your PC. So please forget what you learnt about red being a primary colour – we use magenta as do all printers.

This basic colour wheel consists of 12 colours:
- 3 primaries: yellow, magenta and blue
- 3 secondaries (mixed from the 3 primaries): orange, green and violet,
- 6 tertiaries (mixed from the primaries and secondaries): lime, jade, cobalt, amber (yellow-orange), red and purple.

HUES, TINTS & SHADES

In order to see the relationships at a glance, in this design the primaries are more heavily weighted than the secondaries, which are in turn larger than the tertiaries. Another advantage is that the spaces between the gradated petals are evenly divided in order to accommodate in a tint, a shade and an earth tone or neutral colour for each of the 12 hues. For this colour wheel, we call each true colour of the 12 used, the **hue** of that colour.

This wheel has a space for each hue to have a **tint** where white is added. Many degrees of tints can be obtained, depending on how much white is added. If opaque white is added, the tints will instantly be very light, and can be painted over any dark colour, as they are now opaque and are pastel tones. Clear extender base and white pigment (transparent) can also be added to get pale tones or pastels.

Shades have black added to the hue. Add a minute quantity of black at a time to any colour you need to shade. Just touch the black paint with the tip of your brush when mixing it into the hue. If you add too much, all your shades will look exactly the same – dark charcoal grey! Go easy – rather add more if the colour doesn't look dark enough. This rule applies to all colour mixing.

Hints

- Always add tiny quantities of dark colour to larger quantities of light colour, in other words mix from light to dark. This way, you can keep adding the darker colour until the right colour intensity is obtained. If you do it the other way round you will end up with much more paint than you need.
- To remember what a tint is, think *it* – l*i*ght, wh*i*te, t*i*nt; to remember what a shade is, think *a* – bl*a*ck, sh*a*de, sh*a*pe

Earth tones and neutrals

To bring in earth tones (variations of brown) or neutral colours, we mix each hue with its complementary colour – colours which are found directly opposite each other on the wheel, namely: yellow and violet; magenta and green; blue and orange; lime and purple; jade and red; cobalt and amber.

Complementary colours are a good choice for contrast when selecting colour combinations for painting. To change the tone of a hue from bright and sharp to muted and earthy add small quantities of its complementary colour, for example:

blue + small amount of orange = teal

Mixing together complementaries is also a quick way to obtain brown. There are specific suggestions on mixing various browns in the instructions for the colour wheel project (see page 37).

Intensity

Intensity refers to depth of colour. For instance, yellow seems a less intense colour than blue – but dark amber-yellow which is loaded with bright pigment will be much more intense than the palest of sky blues.

When you buy ready-mixed paints you may find they vary in intensity according to manufacturer or even colour batch. If you mix your own colours from pigments and bases, use accurate measuring equipment to ensure that the intensity of different batches remains the same.

Portfolio bag

You will need

Fabric for portfolio bag (black denim or what you prefer)

Colour wheel template (see page 160) enlarged to 45 cm diameter

Pre-washed and ironed white cotton in these sizes: 52 x 52 cm; 30 x 30 cm; 25 x 30 cm; 3 of 10 x 25 cm; 10 x 35 cm; 15 x 35 cm

HB pencil or tailor's pen with water-soluble ink

7 plastic spoons (one for each primary and secondary and one for extender)

5 identical clean white medium-sized polystyrene palettes (meat and vegetables are packed in these)

Ice cream sticks for mixing

Permanent black marker

Paint: transparent yellow, blue, magenta; opaque white, black

Extender

Medium-sized brushes

Small brush

Narrow masking tape

Applicators

Materials to sew bag

This is a great project for any fabric painter. It's a very useful storage item with the added bonus of displaying your basic paint-mixing and colouring information on it. The bag consists of two large squares of denim sewn into a simple tote bag with handles – large enough to accommodate a 60 x 60 cm sticky board and a folded wad of fabric for painting. Before stitching the two squares together, the completed colour wheel is sewn onto one side to make a big handy pocket in which you can store designs, patterns, stencils, extra fabric or any similar folded flat items.

On the other side, various colour mixing strips are sewn horizontally or vertically according to function to form different sized pockets for small containers of glue, pigments, glitters, liners, brushes, pens, rulers, craft knives, scissors and so on. This side also has two larger pockets – one a square, depicting the steps to create dimension (just big enough for something snackable) and the other a colour-mixing recipe chart, exactly sized to accommodate a copy of this book. Adjust the sizes to suit your equipment needs.

THE COLOUR WHEEL

Trace the pattern onto the 52 x 52 cm fabric and smooth the fabric onto the board or other working surface, ready for painting. If you don't want your labelling to show, use a tailor's pen with water-soluble ink.

Once the wheel is completely painted and dry, you can outline the design neatly with the permanent maker – this hides any messy outlines and defines each colour in its own space.

HINT

Wash and keep your marked palettes for future quick mixing after painting the wheel.

Primaries

Use the black marker to divide a palette into nine even blocks and label the top row *hues*, the middle row *tints* and the bottom row *shades*.

Mix all the hues, tints and shades on your palette before painting them into their designated areas to minimize washing your brush after each colour change.

HUES: Put 2,5 ml (½ t) each of yellow, magenta and blue into the corresponding blocks in the top row on your palette.

TINTS: Put 2,5 ml (½ t) of extender into each block in the middle row. Use an ice-cream stick and mix very little of each hue into the extender to create a lighter colour or tint. If you have added too much colour and the tint is too similar to the hue, add a touch of opaque white and you will have instant pastel. Opaque white is so much denser than transparent extender that it is more effective at lightening a hue quickly. As it turns the paint opaque, it is not suitable for all applications and effects, but it is fine for the colour wheel tints.

SHADES: Put 2,5 ml (½ t) each of yellow, magenta and blue into the corresponding block in the bottom row. Add the tiniest smidgeon of black to the yellow paint and mix. It should be dark or dirty yellow and not green. If it is too dark, wipe the yellow shade block clean with toilet paper and begin again using an even tinier smidgeon of black until you get the right shade. Because yellow is the least intense colour on the palette and black the most intense the balance is very fine.

As you continue mixing shades you will notice the role of colour intensity. You will need progressively more black to shade magenta and even more to shade the more intense blue. The ratio of dark to light increases as the intensity of the colour increases.

Once you've mixed the primaries palette, paint the demarcated areas using a medium-sized brush to fill in large areas and a small brush for the corners.

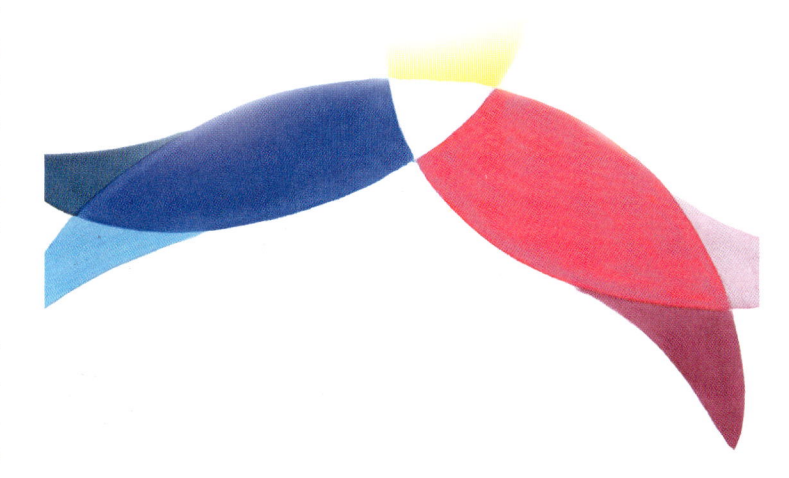

The three demarcated areas for hue, tint and shade and the centre overlap triangle form what looks like the body of a fish. The centre triangle is the head (which will become brown), the petal-shaped body is the hue and the tail fin is split into a shade and a tint. Paint each hue into its marked petal shape, each tint into the adjoining triangle marked (t) and each shade into the adjoining triangle marked (s). To minimize brush wiping and washing between colours, paint in the tint of yellow first, followed by the hue and lastly the shade. Clean the brush well with toilet paper and water before changing hues. You don't want any yellow left in the bristles contaminating the magenta. Also, make sure the brush is dry before proceeding with the next hue – wet brushes can cause the paint to run or bleed.

Leave the middle and final earth-tone triangles (c) open at this stage. You need to have mixed all the hues to be able to proceed with these.

SECONDARIES

Use the black marker to divide the next palette into nine even blocks and label the palette as before. Now mix the secondary hues:

orange	green	violet
4 yellow + 1 magenta	2 yellow + 1 blue	2 magenta + 1 blue

These formulae are approximations and are not cast in stone. If you mix a strong, intense yellow with a weak magenta you may want to change your ratio for orange to 3 yellow + 2 magenta. Gauge the correct amount according to the colour you require.

To mix these hues, use more or less uniform blobs off a teaspoon of each primary hue. Mix a fair amount of each of these secondary colours as you will need them to mix tertiary colours and complementary colours for the wheel. Mix and paint the tints and shades in the same way as for the primary colours palette.

TERTIARIES

Because there are six tertiary colours, you will use two palettes, mixing primaries and secondaries.

Tertiaries 1

As before, the palette is divided and labelled with the word *tertiaries* instead of primaries or secondaries, and these colours.

lime	jade	cobalt
2 yellow + 1 green	1 green + 1 blue	1 magenta + 1 blue

Tertiaries 2

This palette is divided and labelled with the word tertiaries and these colours.

amber	red	purple
3 yellow + 1 orange	1 magenta + 1 yellow	2 magenta + 1 violet

Mix and paint the tints and shades in the same way as the primaries and secondaries.

Hint

If you have bought enough of the primaries to do more than this project, use the formulae to mix extra small tubs of secondary colours which you can store for future use. This way you ensure that the colour batch you have mixed corresponds with your reference wheel.

EARTH TONES

You have to have mixed all 12 hues before doing the earth tones, as it requires you mixing each of them with its opposite or complementary hue. Using the black marker, divide the last palette into 12 even blocks and label it as follows:

yellow + violet	violet + yellow	lime + purple	purple + lime
magenta + green	green + magenta	jade + red	red + jade
blue + orange	orange + blue	cobalt + amber	amber + cobalt

Using the leftover hue colours, (not tints and shades), from your four palettes, put 2,5 ml (½ t) of each hue into the marked blocks.

Add a minute quantity of the complementary colour, just enough to change the hue, to a subtle earthy tone, almost the same as when you were creating the shades by adding tiny quantities of black. You can always add more if the contrast between the hue and its complementary is not great enough. You don't want to end up with mud.

Starting with magenta, for example, moisten your medium brush with green paint and mix into the magenta block. The amount of paint on your brush should be just enough to change the magenta to an earthy tone of magenta – maroon. If your have too much green, the colour will become a greyish brown colour known to us as 'gunge'. Mix and paint in each earth tone triangle in this manner.

Share a secret

Use the flat edge of the brush sideways along the edge of the design to paint a neat edge.

BROWN

Mix any colour with its complementary in more even amounts and you will get varying shades of brown. Do this carefully and label your brown with the quantities used so that you can make them again. For example 10 ml (2 t) yellow to 2,5 ml (½ t) purple. Adjust your mix according to the kind of brown required.

- A rich reddish brown will be obtained by having more of the yellow and red and less blue.
- Khaki will have mostly yellow, with a small amount of red and slightly more blue.
- A dark chocolate brown will be mostly red with yellow and blue in equal quantities and a small amount of black added.
- For fawns and beiges add small amounts of brown tones to extender or white.

Mix a medium brown from orange with purple and violet to paint into the overlap triangle in the middle of your wheel.

Experiment carefully and label your results, bearing in mind when you follow the formulae at a later stage that different batches of primaries may not have the same intensity. It is difficult to reproduce exactly the same colours when you're not using laboratory-exact equipment, so be flexible and experiment.

Allow the painted colour wheel to dry completely, heat set using one of the methods suggested on page 28 and sew onto one side of the portfolio bag to form a pocket.

COLOUR AND DIMENSION

These samples are made into seven pockets of various sizes, and sewn onto the other side of the bag.

Dimension

If you colour in a circle with pure orange hue only, it won't have the spherical appearance of a ball or a fruit or a plate. Shadows and light must be added to give it specific dimension and shape. Shadows and light are created by using tints and shades.

Divide the 30 x 30 cm fabric into four squares with narrow masking tape. Draw a circle in the centre of each square. Paint the circle orange and the background blue in all four squares. Leave the top left square as is.

In the remaining squares, add a white highlight on the top left side of the orange circle. In the bottom squares add a shadow on the right side of the orange using blue paint (complementary colour to orange) curving it to show the shape of a ball. In the bottom right square, also paint a dark shadow against the curved and shaded shape of the ball on the blue background using orange paint (complementary colour to blue) and black (shade colour). This darker shadow of the ball lifts the ball off the background and gives the picture its three-dimensional look.

ric. This is only a guide, however, and may vary with the different makes of paint. Our colour names may also differ from yours, so it may be trial and error. If you want an opaque colour, use opaque base, or white instead of extender.

It's a good idea to keep a record of what you do – a kind of recipe file. If you need the same colour again it is much easier to get as close as possible the next time. A good way to do this is to use calibrated syringes. Record the millilitres of each colour that you use, keep a painted sample and the recipe in your file and you will

Colour recipe chart

To make life a little easier for you, we've included a colour grid to help you mix your favourite colours. Paint it on a 25 x 30 cm rectangle of fab-

cut your work drastically the next time you need the same or a similar colour. The grid works on a ratio system (see page 144).

Black gives a grey shade to the hue and should always be used very sparingly. Take care when you mix hues where all three primaries are needed, or complementaries – you may end up with brown. Add smaller amounts of each colour – you can always add but you can't take out! You will find that two hues often have the same mix of colours, but in different proportions. If you want to make a colour darker add a little of the complementary colour, for example add a little red to green, literally just a drop at a time. To lighten any of these colours, add small amounts of your mixed colour to extender, until the desired colour is obtained. Fill in your own recipes in the spaces provided.

Colour strip pockets

Paint three vertical colour strips of 10 x 25 cm as an exercise in mixing variations of secondary colours:

- yellow and magenta mixed to orange which has more or less magenta and yellow added for a gradation of colour harmony;
- yellow and blue mixed to a harmony of greens;
- blue and magenta mixed to a harmony of purples.

Black to grey to white pocket

On a horizontal strip of 10 x 35 cm, paint a gradation of tints and shades from black through to grey and white by adding white to black or vice versa.

Brown to beige to cream pocket

Use one of a complementary pair of colours – in this case orange and blue – applied to a horizontal strip of 15 x 35 cm to show tints of the mixture from brown through to beige and cream.

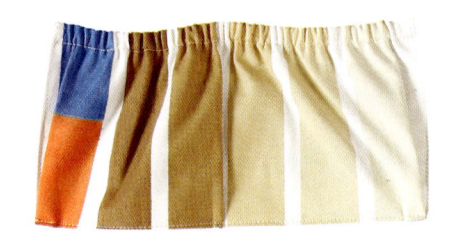

Heat set all the pockets, finish the edges and sew into place on the other side of the portfolio bag as shown on the photograph of the finished bag. Top stitch some of the vertical pockets into smaller divisions to hold brushes and other smaller items before joining

DIRTY PINK
LIGHT SKIN
MED SKIN
DARK SKIN
JACARANDA
DENIM
TEAL
NAVY
GREY
CREAM

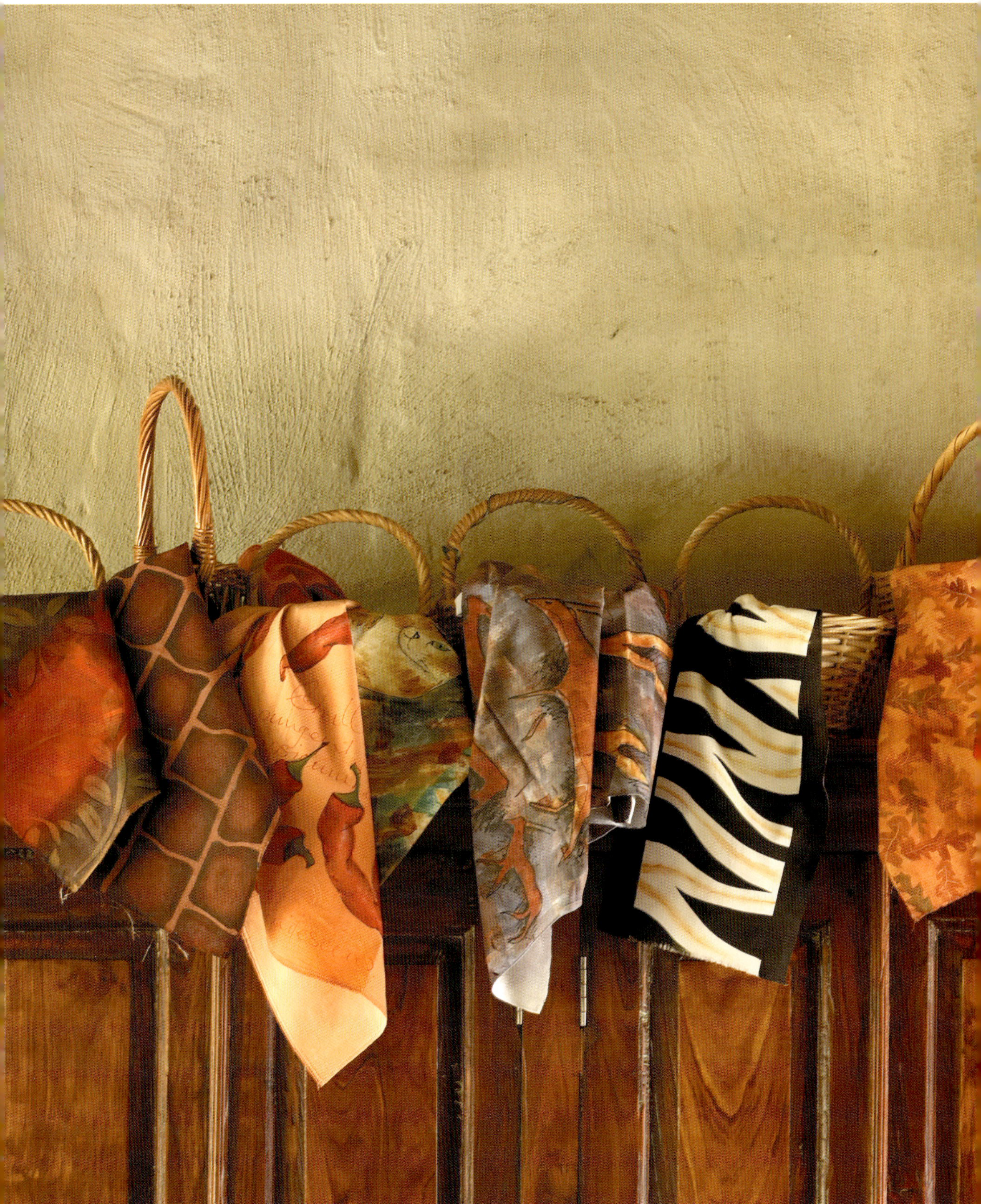

We've explored some popular techniques here and have added many new discoveries, shared many secrets and even confessed to sins committed in our quest. The main techniques included are shading, texture and liners, stripes, checks and tartans, stamping and printing, photo transfer, stencilling, liquid paint, bleaching, simple screen-printing and what to do if things don't go according to plan – yes, there's a very definite technique to that!

Each technique has been illustrated by means of step-by-step projects, and the gallery pages in between include several more finished items with brief descriptions of how that particular effect was achieved. We had great fun putting this together – have fun doing some exploring of your own!

shading

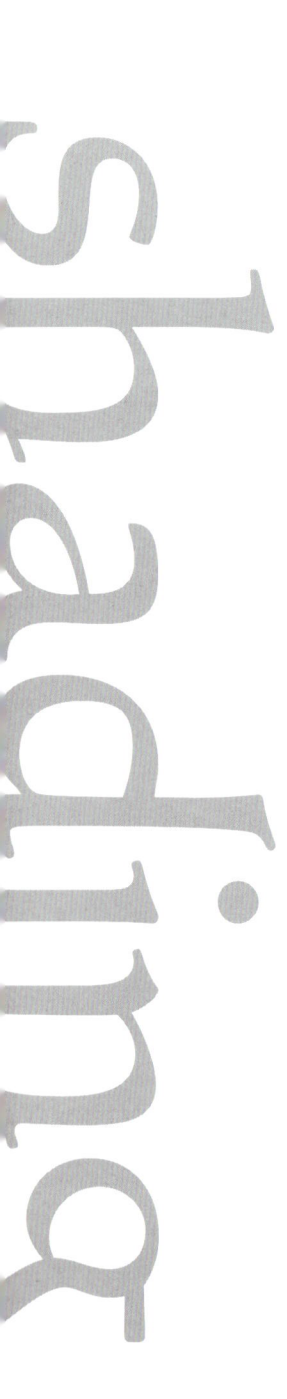

The simplest form of fabric painting is to draw the design in marking pen and to block in colour where needed with a brush or sponge. There are also silkscreen designs available that can be coloured in (similar to 'paint by numbers'). Details can be added with a liner bottle.

To create a more three-dimensional effect, you need to add shading, usually with a darker colour achieved by adding either a small amount of black or the complementary of the colour you are using.

There are several of ways of adding shading. The trick is to be consistent. First determine where the light on your painting is coming from: if the light is coming from the left, the shadows or shading will be on the right. You can wait until your initial painting is dry and then add the darker colour. With this method you have to take care that you work lightly, making things darker as you go, or you could end up with a dirty-looking design.

A good way to add shading is to work into the paint while it is still wet. When painting a flower, for example, you could paint the darker shade onto the wet lighter shade, either from the centre out to create a sense that the flower is going down in the middle, or along one edge of each petal.

Sometimes a combination of these methods works best – shading into the still wet paint and then creating really dark shades when the paint is dry.

Shaded face

Although this design calls for advanced shading techniques, you can simply follow the steps to paint the face on traditional isikaka fabric. Create a beautiful Xhosa shawl by embellishing the fabric with rows of black stitching, braid and buttons.

Isikaka is a heavy-weight woven cotton fabric available in a variety of colours as well as black, white and cream. It drapes and washes and wears well and is very easy to fringe. Wash and rinse thoroughly to remove the size and preshrink it before painting and sewing. If you cannot find isikaka, use soft, heavy cotton curtaining which frays easily so that you can fringe it. Or even sew a ready made fringe onto a good quality calico or seed cloth.

1 Trace the design onto the middle of the shawl fabric.

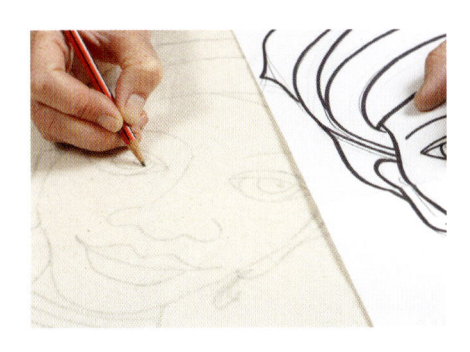

2 Paint the face and neck and little bits of ears with the lightest skin tone. Leave the eyes blank. While the paint is still wet, work the darker skin-tone into all the edges of the face rounding it slightly. Work the colour between the eyelids and brows, and under the nose, cheekbones, lips and chin. Rub the paint in with your finger to give a smooth transition of colour. Before the colour dries, use the dark brown on a medium to fine brush and start blending and defining it into the upper lip, under the lower lip, around the edges of and under the nose, on and between the eyebrows and under the chin fading down the neck on one side.

3 Leave the face to dry and then paint in the irises of the eyes with the dark brown. Also paint in the upper lip and nostrils, defining them carefully. The paint is immediately absorbed and stays dark as you are working onto dry cloth. This works well for definition.

4 Paint a largish pupil into each eye with black paint onto the brown. Using a fine brush and dark skin-tone, paint

You will need

150 x 60 cm isikaka or suitable fabric
Design enlarged to size (see page 155)
Pencil
Materials for finishing
Paint: transparent: light brown, skin tone, medium-brown skin tone, dark brown, black
Liners: black, opaque white and orange

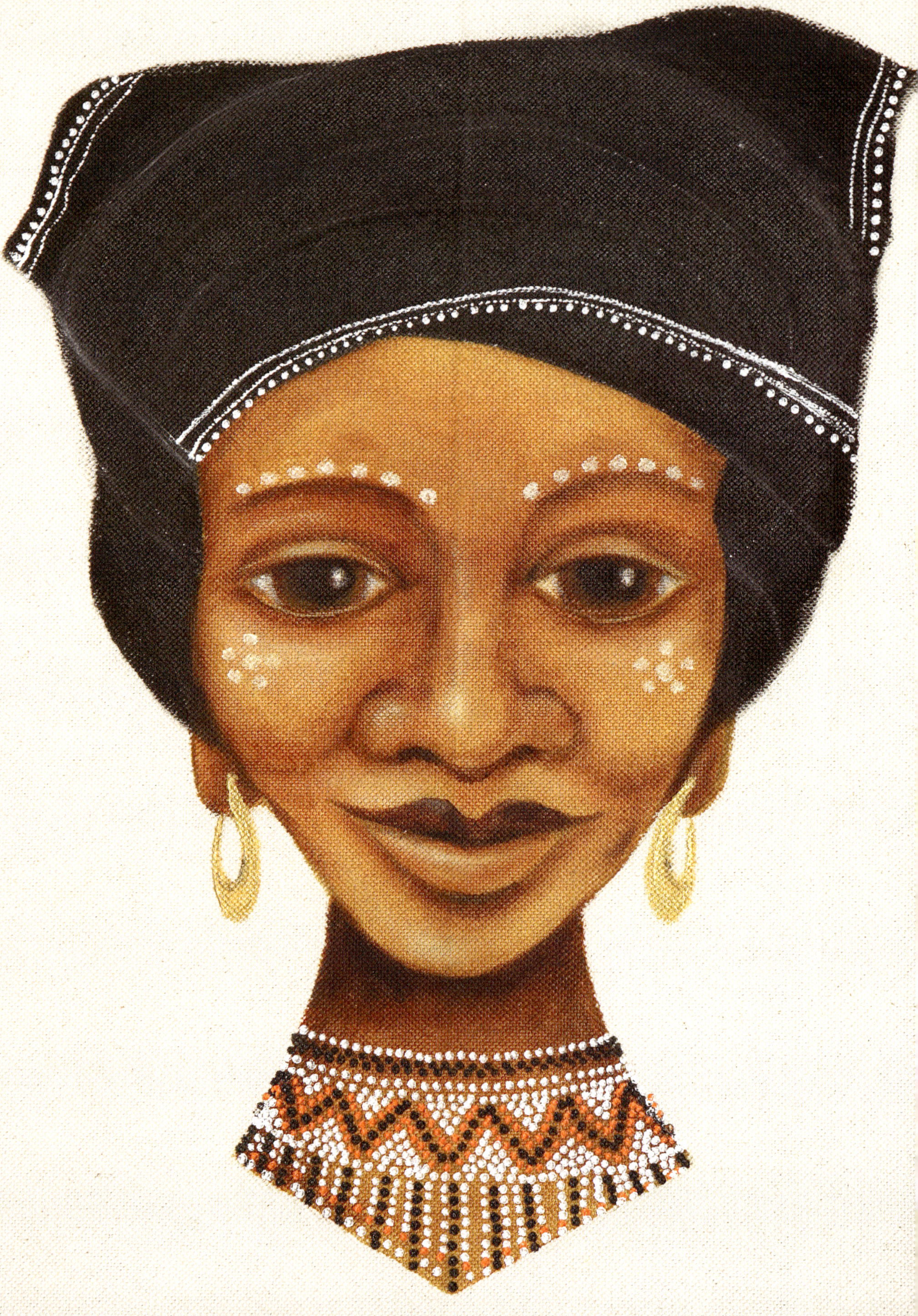

the eyelids over the top of the eye cutting into the irises and pupils and taking up some of the darker wet paint from them onto the lids. This softens the eyelids and makes the irises look more natural. Make sure the pupils are not too small or facing in different directions. Use the sharp wooden end of a brush to impress a highlight spot into the same side of each pupil. If this doesn't show up enough when the paint is dry, add a highlight with a little dot of cream or white paint.

5 Lightly dry-brush the dark colour onto the eyebrows in the direction of growth (from the nasal bridge outwards) to define them.

6 Darken the ear tips with brown and blend more dark brown under the chin for a shadow. This gives your Xhosa princess a regal air and eliminates any possibility of a double chin – which looks great on a fat lady, by the way! Leave to dry well.

7 Paint in the highlights of the headdress with opaque white from the liner bottle. While this is still damp, paint over the entire headdress in black. The highlighted areas should blend in as grey. This is useful for seeing the shadows and also for demarcating the lines where you will use white liner on black to embellish the headdress.

8 Using the coloured, black and white liners, outline the white braiding and black and white and coloured beading on the headdress and necklace with lines and dots to represent braids and traditional beads. Practise on a scrap of cloth to get the feel of the process, working from top to bottom and left to right (or right to left, if you are left-handed). This is a good habit to acquire in painting to avoid smudging your work. Keep a piece of kitchen towel handy for wiping the liner nozzles as you go – otherwise paint builds up around the tip and it gets messy.

9 Dry and heat set the face carefully before sewing and fringing the shawl.

Hints

- It is easier to blend dark colours into light when the base colour is still damp. Mistakes are also easier to correct by simply wiping out carefully with a dry sponge or brush.
- Use a press cloth for heat-setting so that the painted beading doesn't stick to the iron.
- Use fresh liner for a special project.

Shaded cherries

The cherries on this cushion have been carefully shaded, even though the overall effect is definitely red. Painting this design is an excellent exercise in using varying shades of the same basic colour to achieve quite stunning results.

You will need

50 x 50 cm white fabric for painted front
Small to medium flat brushes
Design enlarged to size (see page 147)
Pencil
Paint: transparent orange, red, magenta, pink, burgundy, purple, pale leaf-green, dark emerald
Materials to make up a cushion

1 Trace the design in pencil.

2 Decide where the highlights should be (all towards the same side), and paint them in with a dry brush using red (see page 62 for the dry-brush technique).

3 Paint around these highlighted areas with a combination of red, orange, magenta and pink. Change the combination slightly for each cherry to add more interest. While the paint is still wet shade with a darker red, burgundy and a little purple. The cherries further down in the bowl will naturally be darker, so your initial reds will have to be a little darker and the shading deeper still. You can also add green to your reds to achieve depth. Navy and purple add even more depth.

4 If you feel that the shading is not dark enough, you can add more shading once the cloth is dry.

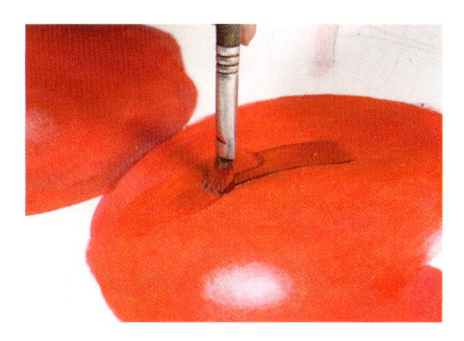

5 Paint in the stems using green.

6 Add red to the green and blend to obtain a deeper shade, and darken the stems along one edge.

7 Allow to dry completely, heat set and sew the cushion.

techniques

Shaded olives

Not all shading needs to be careful and precise. Wonderful textural effects can be created by lifting two or three harmonious colours onto your brush and 'slopping' them onto the cloth, making use of the brushstrokes. The hopsack I used for this olive cloth really lends itself to these textures. This is a great cloth to paint for the messier amongst you! Make some olives green, some purple and others graded from green into purple to add interest.

You will need

Cloth cut to size and overlocked
Medium to large flat brushes
Design enlarged to size (see page 147)
Pencil
Paint: transparent magenta, brick red, purple, pale leaf-green, leaf green, pale grey-green, dark grey-green, earthy green (add red), amber, light amber, brown
Liner brush or brown liner

1 Trace the design in pencil.

2 Start painting the green olives by dry-brushing (see page 62) highlights to one side and just below where the stalk goes into the olives.

3 Pick up two different shades of green and paint in the rest of the olive, using rough brushstrokes without trying to blend the colours too much.

4 Repeat for the purple olives using purple, red and magenta after dry-brushing the highlights. For olives graded from green to purple, take special care not to blend the greens and purples too much, as you will end up with mud.

5 The leaves are filled in with lighter tones of green on one side of the leaf and darker tones on the other. A dry-brush highlight can be left in the middle of the lighter side of the leaf. For variation, I have used two different greens for the leaves.

6 Paint the background by picking up two shades of amber with a large brush and paint in a criss-cross fashion, around the olives.

7 Add the stems using a thin liner brush or brown liner. Outline the olives and leaves, either with a brush or with brown liner.

Hint

To create a border without white tape lines, paint in the entire background first. Allow to dry, tape and paint the border in the same colour as the background.

Opaque shading

You need to use opaque paint for it to show up on dark fabric. Shading with opaque paint can be handled in completely different ways. This project combines stamping and shading with opaque paint, so you don't need a design or to be able to draw. Potato bags make good gifts – use black or a dark coloured fabric to prevent the potatoes sprouting.

You will need

White chalk
35 x 150 cm black cotton drill cut in half lengthways
2 potatoes
Craft knife
Polystyrene palette
Painting sponges
Medium and fine brushes
Bamboo skewer
Paint: opaque white, brown, yellow, blue; transparent black, green, purple
Liner: opaque green, light brown/beige
Extender

1 Using chalk, draw an oval where you will stamp the potato shapes. Draw a triangle a little above it where you will stamp the leaves. Draw a short line leading up from the centre of the oval to join the middle of the base of the triangle. This is your design area.

2 Use the opaque green liner to draw in the stems of the potato plant branching up from the short line in a symmetrical pattern into the triangular leaf area. Leave to dry.

3 Cut the potatoes in half lengthways. Cut as straight as you can as the cut surface will be used as a stamp. From one half cut two or three different leaf shapes and two or three simple star shapes for flowers. Use the tip of the knife to draw vein lines into the flat potato leaf surfaces.

4 Mix the opaque yellow and blue to get a variety of greens. Sponge the green paint onto the carved leaf stamp and stamp these onto and around the stems in the chalked triangle as you would imagine them growing from the stem. Check which direction you have cut the vein lines and make sure they point the right way too. When the stamped opaque green leaves are dry enough, shade them with transparent green and purple. Use purple to make leaves under others appear to have shadows on them. Allow to dry.

5 Stamp flowers over leaves at sparse intervals using opaque white on the carved star-shaped stamps. When these are dry brush them with extender and paint a little transparent purple in the centre with two or three dots of opaque yellow liner for stamens.

6 Mix a sandy brown colour using the opaque white and a little brown paint. Sponge onto the potato halves and stamp them in an overlapping pattern in the chalked oval. Draw in the hair roots with the light brown/beige liner. Leave to dry.

8 Stamp the flat end of the bamboo skewer into the still wet paint to mark potato 'eyes' and use the point of the skewer to draw in creases and prick freckle spots. Heat set after curing for a few days, and sew the potato bag.

7 Block the foreground potatoes in completely with the same colour using a brush. Paint the background potatoes just up to the edges of the foreground ones leaving a shadow between. Using extender and transparent black paint, shade the edges of and shadows between the potatoes.

Shaded strelitzia

This design is particularly striking on dark fabric which calls for the use of opaque paint. The flat opaque colours are shaded subtly with transparent paints to achieve a more natural, three-dimensional effect.

You will need

Black fabric
Design enlarged to size (see page 151)
White chalk
Soft pencil for tracing
Medium and fine paint brushes
Gold milky pen
Paint: Opaque yellow, orange, blue, white; transparent orange, green, purple

1 Trace the design onto the cloth by rubbing chalk over the back of the paper and tracing the design with a soft pencil (see page 26).

2 Block in the petals in opaque yellow and orange.

3 Mix bright green from opaque yellow and a little opaque blue and block in the leaves and stem. Allow to dry.

4 Paint the stamens in opaque blue.

5 Shade over the dry opaque flat colours using the transparent paint. Work transparent orange over the dried yellow and orange. Add shading with transparent green and purple to give dimension to the petal shapes.

6 Paint transparent purple over the dried blue stamens.

7 Use opaque white mixed with transparent orange or yellow to create highlights in the petals.

8 Paint transparent green over the dried opaque green leaves and stem. Use opaque white mixed with transparent green or purple to create highlights in the leaves and stems. Use the transparent orange and purple to shade the leaves and stem creating a three-dimensional effect.

9 After it has air-dried for a few days, sign your painting with its botanical name as well as your own name using a gold milky pen.

The lilies in these designs have been painted onto a textured background using various shading techniques. Darker colours look more dramatic on the cushions, in contrast to the softer finish of the cloth. Note the colour variations of the pale background, where purple and blue were clouded together. A light colour was applied to the leaves as a base before adding the darker greens. The veins were then scratched in while the paint was still wet.

A friend who needed cheering up – and something for her bathroom – was the inspiration for this lush lady, photographed in an exquisite bathroom with a bath many times the size of the bath in the picture! I used mostly transparent paints in this picture, with the exception of the bubbles and the bath. In both instances I shaded white over extender, adding shades of grey and purple for detail and depth. A sea sponge with opaque white speckled more texture on the bubbles. The curtain detail was created by stamping off with a bought leafy stamp.

LEFT I adapted and personalised this shell from a large, busy, shell-collage in a book, as a sample to teach shading and depth using paint on damp extender and a dry background. For three years it was stuck on my workroom wall amidst all the samples until one day I found this battered old frame (ready 'distressed'!) and the two were meant to be together. Each shows off the other's calm simplicity.

BELOW LEFT When Bernie Millar painted this young boy she calls Burdaso, she used oil-painting techniques to bring the portrait to life. It is a copy of a funerary portrait of a young boy on an Egyptian sarcophagus of the 2nd Century AD. The original is currently housed in the Metropolitan Museum of Art in New York.

BELOW RIGHT A very dramatic effect was created with a variety of reds, orange and opaque white. Believe it or not, this rose is exactly the same as the rose used for the stencilled bolster (see page 103). The pattern was enlarged, squared off and – voilà – a new look!

shading gallery

57

texture

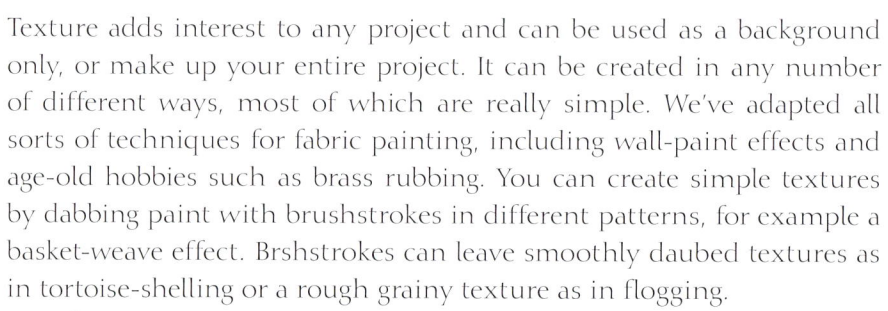

Texture adds interest to any project and can be used as a background only, or make up your entire project. It can be created in any number of different ways, most of which are really simple. We've adapted all sorts of techniques for fabric painting, including wall-paint effects and age-old hobbies such as brass rubbing. You can create simple textures by dabbing paint with brushstrokes in different patterns, for example a basket-weave effect. Brshstrokes can leave smoothly daubed textures as in tortoise-shelling or a rough grainy texture as in flogging.

By first painting an area with extender or a very light colour, you can create really subtle effects, especially for backgrounds. Work into this with darker paint on a brush or a sponge, either in one colour or blending colours as you go. The initial layer provides a smooth surface which facilitates blending, and lightens the colours used. You can create beautiful cloudy effects using a sponge in circular motion. This is similar to colour washing, but results in a smoother texture than colour washing which leaves brushstrokes. If you make a mistake it is easy to erase by wiping over with a clean sponge while the paint is still wet. We use this technique often, in a number of variations.

Dabbing paint onto the area to be coloured with a sea sponge or scrunched up plastic bag, bubble wrap or paper creates a speckled, granite effect. This can be done repeatedly and with a number of different colours or shades of the same colour. If two colours are applied, one on top of the other, the applicator can be used to take off the top colour, creating a different effect.

Scraping with a credit or similar card (old phone cards are great), paint scraper, hard cardboard, spatula, squeegee, and so on, gives lovely textural effects. It is a great way to fill a space quickly and can also be used for making checks and tartans (see page 85).

We also included liners under texture, as they can be used to create optical illusory effects by tightly dotting or spiralling colour onto cloth.

A study in textures

When teaching, we use variations on this bowl of flowers to show students how easy it is to make a picture with textures. You definitely do not have to be an artist to do this, so jump right in and have fun. Experiment with other 'found objects', as we certainly couldn't include all options here.

1 Trace the design with a pencil or blue pen on the right-hand side of the fabric so that the completed design will be on the front of the book once it's made up into a cover. There's no need to trace all the details – you just need a guide. If you are using a background, add that to the entire cloth before painting the design, or fill it in afterwards. We used clouding (see page 117).

2 Stamp the largest shape. Using bubble wrap or a sponge, pick up a small amount of magenta paint and lightly stamp textured marks in the appropriate spaces. Repeat with burgundy, more to one side than the other and then repeat with a little opaque white on the opposite side for highlights.

3 For the rose shapes, use a bunched up sponge and three colours (pink, magenta and violet): place a drop of each of the three colours onto your palette. Dip the sponge into the paint, wipe off gently or dab onto a spare piece of cloth as it should not be too wet. Dip a corner of the sponge into opaque white and twist the paint onto the fabric. Scratch spirals into the wet paint with the end of a brush.

You will need

Fabric to make up a cover for a telephone directory
Design enlarged to size (see page 152)
Pencil or blue pen
Leaf stamp or sponge/potato cut to simple leaf shape
Bubble wrap, plastic bag or textured sponge
Bath sponges
3 brushes in different sizes
Paint: transparent magenta, pink, burgundy, violet, purple, dark blue, light blue, emerald, earthy green, pale olive; opaque white
Liner: opaque white, transparent green

4 Cut a bath sponge into a small square and tie crosswise with two elastic bands to form four petals. Dip this sponge into the purple paint and wipe before printing onto the fabric. Repeat, but turn the sponge slightly when printing, creating a multi-petal flower. The print will be uneven, but this just adds to the texture.

5 Using the leaf shape and a light green, daub leaf shapes between the flowers and over the top of the vase, not in a straight line. Stamping a second time with the same stamp without re-inking will create a lighter print. Fill in the gaps with a different green, using a medium brush and paint in the lavender stalks using a thin brush and pale olive.

6 Paint some clear extender onto the middle left side of the vase. Working into the extender, towards the outside edge, paint in the light blue. Add darker blue towards the edge to create a three-dimensional effect. If you do not want to fiddle too much around the leaves coming onto the vase, leave them out and just have leaves at the top of the vase, underneath the flowers. Sponge in a darker area at the bottom of the bowl so that it looks as if it is standing on a table.

7 Paint the daisy flower shapes with opaque white, this time using the tip of a wider brush to 'print', rather than paint the petals.

8 Make the white dots with liner or by dipping the end of a brush into white and then onto the fabric. Dab purple dots to complete the lavender. The centres of the daisies can also be filled in purple.

9 Outline shapes with liner and draw in a few tendrils, then sign your name with a flourish.

10 Allow to dry, heatset and make up a book cover.

OUTLINING WITH LINERS

Practise on a spare piece of cloth first. You can ruin a good article with bad outlining. If you outline too carefully or too perfectly around the edge of your design, the result looks hesitant, somewhat amateurish and also very stiff. Bolder, sweeping lines, made with confidence in a sketchy manner a little off the design edges, are far more effective, appealing and lively. Don't be too perfect, be interesting! Follow these guidelines when working with liner:

1 Shake the paint in the bottle down into the nozzle end over a piece of scrap or a palette so that all the paint collects in the nozzle with no air bubbles before you start squeezing gently and evenly. Air bubbles will cause your paint to spurt, resulting in uneven lines which will ruin your outline.

2 Hold the liner bottle as upright as possible – if you angle it, paint can blob out in a thick uneven line. Fabric paint is acrylic based which means the thicker it is the more plastic it becomes when dry, and thus susceptible to scorching. Thick outlining takes forever to dry, making it more vulnerable to smudging while wet and sticking to the iron when dry.

3 Make sure the liner nozzle is in direct contact with the cloth as you squeeze the bottle and begin to draw. If not, you will start your line or dot with a blob. When you've completed the line, release the pressure on the bottle before lifting it from the cloth to prevent another blob.

Dry-brushed ball cushion

You will need

Fabric
Large wall brush
Flat punnets
Paint: transparent apricot, red brown
Materials to make up a ball cushion

Dry-brushing is most often used as a highlight when shading a motif. There is almost no paint on the brush, so it's exactly what it says – a dry brush. It can be a wonderful textural effect, hence its inclusion here. It also makes a great background, done over the entire cloth first and then painted over. Make it as light as you wish, or darken by adding more layers.

1 Dip the brush into the apricot paint, scrape off any excess and paint the punnet. Only then draw the brush over the cloth lightly, in a sweeping motion. Keep your touch light. Try to keep the same direction for an even effect. Repeat until the cloth is covered.

2 You may want to cover the whole area again in a different colour and in the opposite direction, like I have done here. Using the same colour in the opposite direction will achieve a different effect. You do not always have to keep painting in a horizontal or vertical direction, but can use a criss-cross motion for an entirely different effect.

3 Allow to dry. Heatset and make up a ball cushion.

Tortoiseshell bolster

A tortoiseshell texture is a lovely, subtle blend of brush daubings in a harmonious colour range. While I painted this bolster cover in traditional tortoiseshell colours, any range of harmonies will do. The peach-skin fabric I used has a soft, velvety feel, ideal for this subtle technique.

You will need

Fabric to make bolster

Medium to large wall-painting brushes

Hake brush (or large soft-bristled brush for softening)

Paint: transparent golden yellow; rust; tan and dark brown with binder medium added if you use synthetic fabric such as peach skin

Materials to make up a bolster cover

1 Paint the cloth golden yellow using a large brush.

2 Daub brush strokes in a diagonal pattern in rust and tan across the damp yellow background using a medium brush. Daubing is like leaving a brush's finger prints on the cloth – you need to load the brush with enough paint to leave a reasonable sized splodge.

3 Soften and blend the paints by brushing softly over the daubings in the same diagonal direction using a large wall-painting brush.

4 Add dark brown markings sparingly and blend in with the hake or softening brush.

5 Heat set when dry and make up a bolster cover.

Flogging

You will need

1 m x 1,5 m fabric
Painting sponge
  or wall-painting brush
Flogging brush
Paint: transparent
  golden yellow, rust,
  tan, dark brown
Extender

Work off your frustrations flogging a brush with fabric paint onto a piece of fabric. Use a large wall-painting brush with long, almost floppy bristles which can slap paint down very satisfyingly onto a wet, painted background. This leaves a hairy, stippled effect, and is a lovely texture simulating animal fur. We made up a looong, lollable cushion in blocks, alternating rectangles of contrasting flogged fabric with satin to break the monotony of a large surface. It was finished with tassels at the corners.

1 Sponge or paint the entire cloth with extender or the lightest colour (or a mixture of extender and one of the colours).

2 Dab the other colours onto the cloth using a sponge – you can do this in layers or patterns or just use one colour.

3 Hold the flogging brush loosely and slap it down lightly and rhythmically all over the cloth, working in the same direction. You will be lifting and transferring colours which will mix and blend subtly, while leaving a hairy, stippled effect.

4 Add more colour as you flog if you find that the wet paint on the wet background mutes the colours too much.

5 Heat set when dry and make up into a cushion.

Wood-grain effect

A wood-graining tool can be bought at most hardware or paint shops. It creates a beautiful wood-grain effect in emulsion wash or fabric paint when combed, dragged and rocked across a prepared, wet-painted surface.

You will need
Fabric
Graining tool
Painting sponge
Wide wall-painting brush
Paint: transparent golden yellow, rust, tan, dark brown
Extender
Materials to make up a cushion cover

1 Sponge the cloth with extender and yellow, streaking the colour in the direction you want the wood grain to go – preferably towards you as this makes working with the graining tool easier.

2 While the cloth is still damp, brush on the rust, tan and dark brown paints in the same direction.

3 Starting at the furthest end of the cloth away from you, pull the graining tool towards you in a rocking and sliding movement over the wet painted surface in the same direction as the brush strokes. Work parallel to the edges of the cloth and repeat the grain effect in parallel lines across the cloth to simulate wooden boards.

4 Heat set when dry and make up a cushion cover.

Dragged book-cover

Perhaps the opposite of dry brushing is dragging – you certainly need a lot more paint. The dragged-lined effect created here as a background for stamping and lining has been achieved with long, continuous brushstrokes across fabric which has been coated in a layer of paint. While we used the fabric for a book cover, this is a really great way to do placemats or small overlays. Attempt a larger cloth only if you have enough space to leave it to dry flat. Once painted, it is best not to move the fabric until the paint has dried, as it will scratch very easily. Hanging it over anything to dry will create a lighter line.

You will need

Design enlarged to size
Wide wall-painting brushes
Stamps
Scratching implement
Sponge
Paint: transparent pale yellow, yellow, orange, red, burgundy
Extender
Black liner

1 Trace the basic pattern in pencil.

2 Sponge the cloth with extender, making sure that it is completely covered. Any gaps will result in a darker paint mark and ruin your work. Adding a little base colour to the extender makes it easier to see.

3 Dip the brush into two different colours and drag it across the fabric. Bear in mind that with transparent paint the colours will blend, for example blue painted over red will show up purple, so don't overwork the colours as you could end up with mud.

4 Continue like this, changing colours as you progress up the fabric. If you do not want to grade your colours, use two or three variations of the same colour, and drag across your fabric in a similar way. As you are working on top of extender the brushstrokes will be visible. If your work is patchy, simply drag your brush lightly from one side to the other. This creates the dragged effect.

5 Scratch the design into the wet paint with the back of a brush or eraser or other implement. You can also use the end of a paintbrush, the thin end of a clothes peg, an old fork, a hair comb or whatever you have to scratch the design into the wet paint.

6 Stamp off where required, using stamps of your choice. We used two different stamps and the cap of a white-board marker.

7 Leave to dry and add further details with liner.

8 Leave to dry thoroughly, heat set and make up book cover.

IMPRESSING

A variation on this theme is to paint a solid colour onto one piece of fabric and then to lay another piece of fabric on top. Scratch a design onto the fabric and when lifted, the top fabric will have a line drawing, while the bottom fabric will have an etched look. The one is opposite to the other.

Rubbing

You will need

Fabric
Masking tape
Different textures
Sponges and/or brushes
Paint: transparent beige,
  brown, tan,
  pale apricot
Liners: transparent
  beige, red-brown

If fabric is placed over a textured surface, the texture underneath will come through if paint is rubbed over the fabric – much like brass rubbing. Try putting your fabric over a mosaic tiled floor, a plastic garden table, wood with a raised grain – anything with an interesting texture! The type of fabric you use will have an effect on the look of your finished work.

This throw is a very rough linen, so the textures are not as obvious as they would be on a smoother fabric. I used a variety of different textures: a steel plate, garden mesh and a homemade texture of starch made by outlining a leaf shape on a sticky board with a flour and water paste (see resists, page 92, for recipe).

1 Place masking tape around the area that you wish to colour. Place this area of fabric over of the chosen texture.

2 Dip the sponge or brush into the paint and remove all excess paint by scraping the sponge along the side of the container. Excess paint will cause a blob.

3 Gently rub the sponge across the area to be painted, taking care not to move the fabric as this will blur the effect of the rubbing.

4 Repeat in the other areas of the cloth you wish to decorate, changing colour and texture in the relevant sections.

5 If you have used white fabric, you may find that the white shines through your textures too strongly. Sponge a pale colour over the entire cloth to alleviate this.

6 Finish by applying liner to certain sections. Allow to dry and heat set.

Sponged ball-cushion

I just love the idea of ball cushions, so I made two – it brings a whole new bounce to the art of pillow fighting. The granite texture is created by sponging various colours onto the fabric, using a sea sponge. If you are working on white fabric, apply a light colour first to prevent stark white sections jumping out at you and spoiling the effect. I used light beige. If you are making a ball cushion, first paint the cloth in one piece and then cut out the pattern.

You will need

Fabric
Sea sponge (or bag, or bubble wrap)
Paint: transparent beige, taupe, brown.
Opaque white (optional)
Materials to make a ball cushion

1 Apply beige paint to the entire cloth.

2 Dip the sponge into a small amount of taupe paint in a container. Remove excess paint by scraping the sponge along the side of the container. Too much paint will cause a blob, rather than a speckled texture. Lightly dab the paint all over the fabric. Change the direction of the sponge as you go along so that you do not end up with a repeat pattern.

3 Repeat with the brown. If you want a crisp, speckled effect, as we have here, allow the paint to dry between colours. Sponging on wet paint will soften the effect.

4 Lastly dab on opaque white to add highlights (optional). Allow to dry, heat set and make up the ball cushion.

techniques

Bagged cushion with braid

You will need

Fabric
Paper or other scrunchy material (please recycle!)
Paint: transparent pale orange, tan (add binding medium if you are using synthetic fabric)
Sponge
Brush
Materials to make a cushion

Applying two colours, one on top of the other, then using a scrunched up plastic bag, bubble wrap or whatever else you can think to take off some of the top layer of colour, creates a completely different texture, almost the opposite of sponging. I used paper for this project, as it gives a crisper, more definite pattern. Painting the fabric for the cushion was really simple, but it is made quite special by the finishing. I used peach skin for its lovely, soft feel.

1 Using a sponge, coat the entire cloth with the pale orange, making sure you haven't left any gaps. These will cause ugly darker marks when you apply the darker colour.

2 Using either a sponge or a brush, apply the tan paint over the pale colour while the pale colour is still wet.

3 Dab a piece of scrunched paper onto the wet paint lifting it off the fabric. Repeat across the fabric, changing the direction of the scrunched paper as you go to avoid a repeating pattern. Depending on the size of the fabric, you may need to use different sides of the paper, as overuse will make it soggy and smudge the effect. Use fresh paper when necessary.

4 Allow to dry thoroughly, heat set and make up a cushion.

Cushion with faux marble

Yes, you can simulate marble on fabric! Adjust the technique slightly, by adding fewer veins, and you have a rock on which to paint your cave art.

You will need

Fabric
Small, medium and large brushes
Sponges
Feather
Paint: transparent pale orange, tan, red brown, pink brown
Extender
Materials to make a cushion

1 Cover the fabric with extender or very pale orange.

2 Paint tan diagonally onto the wet extender in wavy lines, joining them here and there. Repeat across the cloth, leaving some of the background colour showing through.

3 Soften this pattern by brushing over gently with a sponge or brush. Do this first in the same direction as your lines and then in the opposite direction, slightly blurring them.

4 Repeat the diagonal waves with red brown or a slightly darker or toning colour, filling in more of the background, though still leaving some of the pale colour showing. Soften as before.

5 Repeat the diagonal pattern again, using a thinner brush and a slightly darker colour. Soften again.

6 Slightly water down your darkest colour. Use the feather to drag this across the fabric, twirling the feather as you go. This will create very uneven, interesting veins. You can soften these too and repeat if necessary.

7 Allow to dry thoroughly before heat setting and making up a cushion.

Scraped baskets

For this technique you build up a picture, using a scraper – we used old phone cards, some cut to give us different widths to work with. We used scraping across the entire design but you could scrape either a background or just the motifs. Keep the shapes fairly simple. Dimension can be added, either by shading with transparent paint, as we did here, or by highlighting with a little white which works particularly well with flower motifs. Painting a design like this is a great way to use up leftover paint.

You will need

Fabric
Design enlarged to size (see page 156)
Black fabric pen
Scraping tools of varying widths
Medium brushes
Materials to make up a cushion cover
Paint: transparent orange in various shades, apricot, taupe, maize, grey, red brown, beige
Black liner (optional)

1 Draw the design in black fabric pen.

2 Dip the card into the paint and scrape it onto the fabric. For this design we scraped horizontally and vertically only. Change colour for each shape and leave some fabric peeping through. Use scrapers of different widths as required by the design. Don't worry about going over the lines – we dare you to! It adds to the effect and is *desirable*. Your primary school teacher is not watching.

3 Repeat this again and again, adding more toning colours to each shape. Do try to leave some white otherwise the design will become dull.

4 When you are satisfied, shade around the edges of each basket with a brush to round the shapes and give the work some depth.

5 If you wish, you can add definition and detail to the shapes by adding liner. We have also been very bold and scribbled in some shadows. Don't overdo this, as you may end up with big black splodges. Under-doing it will look scribbled. Practise first!

Hint

Dark liners can add to the drama of a piece, but can spoil it if overdone. So step back and assess your work often.

Cookie-cutter waves

What an effective texture this is! It is really easy to achieve, but can be messy. I used this to great effect for the background of a shopping bag, decorated with lino-stamped butterflies in a darker colour. Stretch your fabric in some way before you start to avoid the frustration of fabric riding up as you drag the cookie cutter across. A lino stamp has a unique appearance and making your own is really easy if you stick to a simple design.

You will need

Fabric (a little larger than you will need for your finished project)
Cookie cutter (or tube).
Paint: transparent pale orange, maize, pale taupe, red brown
Lino
Design (see page 152) enlarged to size and drawn on paper
Pencil
Carbon paper
Basic lino cutting tools
Sponge roller
Materials to sew a shopping bag

1 Place the cookie cutter at one of the top corners and place a blob of each of your colours into it.

2 Gently drag the cutter across the fabric in a straight or wavy line, until you reach the other end of the fabric and pull down a little, ready for the next stripe. Top up with blobs of colour, if necessary, and repeat all the way back across the fabric.

3 Allow to dry and add interest by stamping or painting a motif over the textured background.

4 To make the lino stamp, lay your design onto the lino, over a sheet of carbon paper, and trace the outlines. Using the various cutting tools (practise on a piece of scrap lino first), cut around the design and shave away all the unwanted background. You may want to leave a sliver of background here and there, as this is what gives lino its individual appearance. Warming the lino slightly in the oven or toaster (don't cook it) before you start cutting, softens it and makes it easier to cut.

5 Work out where the stamps are to be placed and mark the fabric accordingly.

6 Apply red brown paint to the lino stamp with a sponge roller, taking care to cover the entire surface without getting too much paint on it.

7 Stamp away. Remember to re-ink before each impression is made.

8 Allow to dry thoroughly. Heat set and sew a shopping bag.

techniques

Malachite effect

You will need

Enough white fabric for cushion front

Stiff cardboard, large enough to hold comfortably in one hand

Painting sponge

Large paintbrush

Small, stiff bristle brush

Paint: transparent dark emerald

Extender

Materials to make up cushion cover

Traditionally this effect is green – like the stone it simulates. For an interesting effect, try it in colours to match your wood-grained cushion cover, like we have done, using transparent golden yellow, rust, tan and dark brown.

1 Mix a pale cucumber green from extender and emerald and sponge this colour onto the cloth evenly.

2 Before the pale green dries, paint over with dark emerald using the wide brush. Paint in swirls and circles holding the brush upright so that it leaves uneven, dragged lines.

3 Score the piece of cardboard down the centre using a craft knife. Do not cut through the score line. Bend along the score line once. Pull apart the two halves along the score line so that it leaves a reasonably straight but hairy edge.

4 Hold the cardboard upright with the hairy edge down onto the wet paint. Drag circular and semi-circular patterns into the wet paint. Create jagged effects as well by pulling the card in small, sharp 'V' shapes while following the dragged curve.

5 Use a small, stiff bristle brush to fix up the centres of circles or tidy up edges.

6 Heat set when dry and make up a cushion cover.

Hint

Cut one half of the torn cardboard in two different widths so that you can make smaller patterns as a variation.

Lapis lazuli

Use paint in shades of the rich, dark blue of the precious stone to create the precious-stone effect on fabric.

You will need
Fabric
Sponge
Bubble wrap (small bubbles)
Large paintbrush suitable for stippling
Feather
Paint: transparent dark, royal blue, violet
Extender
Small, thin brush
Gold dust (gold embossing powder)

1 Mix a light blue colour by adding a little of the dark blue to extender. Using the sponge, rub this light blue over surface of the entire cloth.

2 Apply the royal blue paint in a random honeycomb pattern to your still damp, light blue cloth, using scrunched bubblewrap, dabbing lightly to achieve a sea-sponge effect.

3 Mix some royal blue with an equal quantity of violet to darken it and again use bubble wrap to dab paint into the spaces between the royal blue honeycombing with the darker colour. Overlap the blues to create a sponged effect of drifting dark and light blue textured clouds.

4 Soften the roughness of the bubble wrap sponging by stippling with a large paintbrush. Hold the brush upright and dab the bristles lightly onto the paint – work from the lightest to the darkest patches otherwise you will flatten the colour variation too much.

5 Dip a small, thin brush into the gold dust and spatter over the wet painted blues. Draw gold 'veins' with the same brush dipped in water and gold dust. Use this sparingly for the best effect.

6 Draw a few clean veins through the wet paint using the tip of the feather. For interesting lines, twist and swirl the feather slightly as you draw.

Hint
The gold dust will only adhere to wet paint. Blow off any excess once the paint is completely dry.

techniques

77

Spiralled cushion

You will need

Cotton drill
Light-weight cotton
Medium paintbrushes
Paints: transparent yellow, orange, magenta
Liners: opaque yellow, orange, magenta, gold
Materials to make up cushion

Liners are great for adding texture to your work. Opaque liners are vibrant on dark backgrounds while transparent-based liners show up beautifully on light fabrics. This is a good exercise to try if you find you need to practise outlining. The sweetie cushion is easy to sew and has proved a great hit among teenagers. I used cheeky, bright colours, like those used in sweetie wrappers.

1 Daub splodges of colour randomly onto the cotton drill using medium paintbrushes.

2 Ring the splodges with different colours in the same range.

3 Add more rings of bright colour until they merge and cover the white fabric.

4 Allow to dry well before spiralling bright opaque liners onto and between the base circles of colour. See page 61 for guidelines on neat lining.

Above The main design was created with starch resist, with lots of textural effects. The central background to the cloth has dolphins shadow stencilled onto it for an ethereal effect. Bubbles were stamped off, using the back of a brush and tops of pens. The border has been sea sponged in the same turquoises and blues. This technique is the same as that used in the granite cushion project, but with a totally different look. The shells were also shaded in the same blues and turquoises.

Right Fruit is always popular but I wanted to do something a little different, so I decided to enlarge my design dramatically. I quickly scraped in the basic colours, relevant to each area, using credit cards and larger scrapers. It created magnificent texture. Shading was added with a brush. The blue background is a good foil for such a wide array of colours. Black liner, added quite heavily at the end, really brought out the bright colours.

Left The bunches of grapes were carefully shaded with a brush using various shades of green, orange and purple, to show them in different stages of ripeness. Artistic licence was used in the combination of similar shades for the grapes and leaves. You wouldn't find these colours in the leaves till autumn, when the grapes have long been picked!

The background was clouded in two shades of orange, with a double border masked, and sponged in the darker orange once the paint was dry. A textured detail was added at the end with a 'curly' stencil in the same background orange.

Right A few years ago Dutch artist, Ton Schulten, brought out his first calendar and my classes really enjoyed his images of 'blocked' landscapes. I decided that we needed an African version – with a twist! Using the block idea, I scraped this textured landscape with credit cards and many layers of colours, building up the rich African light. I finally added thin black liner for detail in the trees and huts only. It is difficult to know when to stop with this technique and overworking could spoil it, so it's a good idea to step back from your work often to see how you're progressing.

If you make a mistake while painting or spill dark paint onto a light background, don't throw away your work. We revamped a very mediocre cloth with paint spilt on it into a stunning cover for an ottoman. By adding more layers of paint over a lighter background and then scraping and stamping off you create a magnificent canvas for textures. Drag the paint over the cloth for a dragged background. Once you're satisfied with your design, allow to dry, then add details with liner. You can also stamp on with metallics or darker colours.

A few years ago I decided to make a fun project for each of my boys (Dad included). The fabric for teddy here, and his mates, was washed in shades of pale beiges and oranges and then printed with a homemade sponge stamp to add the texture. Dad's teddy still sits on his desk at work!

An intricate-looking design like this is really simple to do by lining with puff paint for a relief effect. The puff paint was heated under the grill in sections, though the common method is to use a hair dryer on the hottest setting until the paint has puffed. A pale burnt orange was then sponged over the top. The puffed area appears lighter.

texture gallery

These techniques are very useful for filling in backgrounds, as borders or centres of cloths, for placemats, serviettes or backs of cushions. Use colours from your main design in your stripes or checks for an effective matching cloth or backing. The colour and line variations are endless. Create interest by varying colours and textures.

Stripes

Painting stripes is so simple. Try doing them freehand if you have a straight eye, or cheat by first drawing lines with a blue tailor's pen or use a ruler as a guide. When you use masking tape, remember that the spaces between the strips of tape determine the width of the stripes and not only the width of the tape.

Open stripes, where gaps show the original colour fabric between coloured lines, are painted differently from solid stripes where coloured lines abut. For open stripes, lay parallel strips of masking tape onto fabric and paint between the strips. Work excess paint off the masking tape and remove it before the stripes dry. For even, solid stripes, lay masking tape strips against each other. Remove every odd tape and reserve on a clean surface. Paint between the remaining strips. Work excess paint off the masking tape and remove it before the stripes dry. Once the paint is dry, lay the reserved masking tape over the coloured lines and paint between the strips.

Checks and tartans

To paint checks, paint a series of parallel stripes in transparent paint, then paint another series of parallel stripes crosswise over them. Softer, more elegant checks result if you lighten the colours of the second series of stripes with extender. Using two or more colours from your colour wheel results in a more traditional looking check or tartan. For example where transparent blue and yellow stripes overlap on a white background, the crossover block will be green. Add extender to these colours to form lighter pastel stripes of the same colours.

Opaque colours can be used if applied first and then overlaid by transparent colours. They will then take on a different colour. If you use opaque colour last, you will be left with a definite stripe running through your check or tartan, and not achieve a woven, blended look. If this seems in anyway confusing, try the simple, step-by-step instructions for the various projects in this section.

Scraped stripes – hammock

You will need

3 m x 1,5m canvas

Large space to lay out the canvas

Long ruler or straight stick (a broom stick is great – cut in half after painting and use to strengthen hammock ends)

Old phone cards cut in various widths

Tile cement applicators or scrapers

Paint: transparent greens and purples

I used a long ruler and old phone cards to apply the stripes jazzing up a plain canvas hammock. If you prefer something a little more controlled, use masking tape instead as your striping guide and a painting sponge, brush or roller instead of the scrapers.

1 Lay your cloth on a long work surface – on the floor if nowhere else is free.

2 Working parallel to the edges, hold the ruler or stick firmly to guide you as you pull various stripe widths lengthways down the cloth with your scrapers. The scraping should look irregular – this is part of its charm and masks any irregular join when you extend the stripe. Clean your ruler or stick before repositioning. It can transfer a very smudgy line which looks messy.

3 Vary the width of the stripes by using different scrapers, and leave unpainted gaps between the coloured stripes.

4 Allow to dry thoroughly and preferably heat set in an industrial tumble drier – or if you're careful and have enough space, in your home oven. Make up the hammock.

Funky tartan table-runners

Colours that lie next to each other on the colour wheel result in harmonious checks or tartans. If you prefer earth tones, use complementary colours in your basic tartan, for example red and green or yellow and purple. Your overlap colour will be brown, so alternate the colour striping unless you want a finished check of brown blocks. I stuck to the greens and purples for the tablerunners, resulting in soft kaki where the colours overlap.

You will need

30 cm x 1,5m white cotton fabric
Phone cards cut to diferent widths
Small sponge roller
Paint brush
Paint: transparent in two shades of green and two shades of purple
Extender
Liners: green and purple (optional)
Materials to make table runners

1 Scrape alternating green and purple stripes lengthways down the fabric using different widths of phone card. Allow to dry.

2 Add a little extender to the paint and make the cross stripes in varying widths using the roller, paint brush or different width scrapers. Again alternate the colours for maximum colour variation.

3 When the checks are dry, if you wish, draw liners lengthways and crossways over the checks to create a distinctive plaid look.

4 Allow to dry thoroughly, heat set and make table runners.

Hint
If you end up with a particularly dull tartan, lift it by adding gold, white, black or bright liner.

Gingham picnic-basket liner

Gingham is a transparent based, single colour, regular check on a light background. It is the simplest check with which to start. My picnic basket needed something light and cheerful to liven up its looks. I loved the light lime-green used for the hammock and since I had mixed more of that than the other colours it was an obvious choice for the picnic basket. While I was painting this I heard someone say over the radio that lime green was now considered passé in the field of home décor ... Too bad – I like it anyway, and it's just fine for a picnic set.

You will need

Fabric to line a picnic basket (add fabric to line the lining, for useful matching pockets and serviettes)
Narrow masking tape
Painting sponge
Paint: transparent lime green
Extender
Materials to sew a picnic-basket liner

Hint

Did you mask off horizontal and vertical stripes at the same time ending up with blocks? To rescue your check, relay the tape in one direction and re-paint the stripes, allow to dry and repeat the relaying and painting at right angles.

1 Lay strips of masking tape lengthways on your cloth in evenly spaced parallel stripes and smooth the tape down well – no paint should seep under the tape.

2 Sponge the paint evenly *down* the gaps between the masking tape. Wipe the tape strips clean of excess paint which can delay drying time and cause smudging when lifting the tape.

3 Dry thoroughly and lift the tape – the paint must be bone dry or the new masking tape will not adhere properly when you lay it across the painted stripes.

4 Lay new strips of masking tape at right angles across the painted lines, with the gaps between the strips exactly the same as for the painted stripes.

5 Add extender to lighten the paint colour a little and sponge the lighter lime green evenly down the gaps between the tape. The paint will blend with the painted lines, darkening these blocks slightly.

6 Allow to dry and lift the masking tape to reveal your pretty gingham check. Heat set and sew the picnic-basket liner, paying particular attention to the alignment of the blocks. I added useful pockets and decorated some plain white table napkins with a simple handkerchief border check in matching green and contrasting lilac. A homemade stamp put plain purple hearts in the corners, and my picnic hamper lives on.

SOMETHING DIFFERENT

Try the following for adventurous, unusual and easy tartan effects:

- Fill in masked lines with a texture, for example use a sea sponge or scrunched up plastic bag to apply the paint, spray pigment dyes or scratch lines or motifs into the wet painted lines for a textured effect.
- Use a sponge roller to create lines without the use of masking tape. This gives an uneven but interesting effect.
- Paint stripes freehand, with different widths of brushes and uneven brushstrokes.
- Wet your fabric first for a soft bled tartan where the colours are not so definite, but draw more into each other.
- Experiment with wavy lines and liner bottles.
- Try out all your own particular variations of colour, stripe width and texture – use the whole spectrum in one tartan and see what interesting results you get.

INCORPORATING MOTIFS

Mask out the area (motif) that will not be checked or striped using masking tape or a negative stencil and paint stripes or checks around the masked area using any method discussed. Treat the masked area as part of the cloth. Allow to dry well before lifting the masking tape or stencil.

You can also coat motif masks with pressure sensitive (stencil) glue, leave until tacky and place them in position on your unpainted cloth. Then paint in the checked background. When the masks are lifted the blank motif areas can be painted.

Solid check

There are various ways of painting solid checks and it is a great exercise (reinforcing colour theory) to paint this step by step using yellow, magenta and blue resulting in green, blue and purple check. And to practise incorporating motifs, add a loving heart as you go.

I experimented happily making two squares as samples and rather than make another cushion cover turned them into a reversible pocket (the photograph opposite shows the unmasked side) which was sewn onto my daughter's favourite lime-green fleece blankey. It now folds up neatly (instead of lying on the floor) into the pocket for our happy hearts picnic.

You will need

Fabric
Masking tape
Heart stencil negative, primed with stencil glue
Heart stamp (optional)
Paint: transparent: yellow; magenta and blue
Extender
Lightweight fleece blanket
Materials to make blillow

1 Position the heart shape on the centre of the cloth. Stick masking tape strips on either side of the heart, parallel to the edge of the cloth. Paint the centre stripe magenta and the edge stripes yellow. Allow to dry thoroughly.

2 Lift masking tape and the heart negative. Lighten blue paint with an equal amount of extender and paint over the entire cloth. The magenta will become purple, the yellow green, and the white – where the masked strips and heart were – becomes blue. Dry fabric well.

3 Stick new masking tape strips at right angles to the previous rows on the cloth and on either side of the blue heart. These lines can be symmetrical or parallel to each other at random widths.

4 Paint the stripe across the heart in magenta which has been mixed with a little extender to lighten it. This will turn the heart and light blue lines light purple.

5 Paint the other stripes in yellow, and plain and lightened magenta and blue. Use plain magenta and plain blue for the narrow cross stripes as they will overpower the check if used over wide areas. Remask every alternate heart and paint that stripe with a second layer of magenta to render the purple a deeper colour.

6 Remove the masking tape and stamp magenta hearts for an interesting multi-coloured blend effect.

SHARE A SECRET

The three-block check design of the reversable pocket reminded me of noughts and crosses. So, thanks to our friendly carpenter, Peter, we have a hearts and kisses game to play when we picnic. The wooden painted cut-outs double as drinks coasters when you're tired of playing games and when you pack up to go, the pieces tuck away neatly into the channel pockets sewn into the main pocket.

HINT

For the check to stay fresh and appealing and not develop into drab browns, some colours need to be masked out when using the solid check method described here. In order to keep green and purple next to each other without having to put the blue in between, I had to first paint yellow stripes and then mask them out completely by sticking masking tape over them. I could then paint magenta stripes right up against them. When I removed the tape and painted light blue over the cloth my stripes turned into nicely abutting green and purple ones. Thereafter it was easy to paint cross stripes in variations of green, purple and magenta onto this base to create the effect I wanted without the blue.

Experimenting with checks and tartans was such fun I was able to resurrect a mouldering deckchair cover rescued from the depths of a disgraceful garage. A soaking in bleach removed most of the gunge from the canvas and rough checks painted with wide and narrow wall-paint brushes now hide any lingering blemishes. A cover for an old neck bolster was easily made by dabbing random blocks of colour crosswise over each other for further effect. I made the cover reversible by rough-striping the colours on the other side.

The loosely painted fruit with the carefree outline begged for some sort of border and I decided to repeat nearly all the colours in a check. I divided the cloth into eighths and, using the fold lines as a guide, made stripes using a roller. I then painted a stripe in between. I changed colours and widths a few times, filling up the space. As this is a round cloth, the stripes converge towards the centre. For the very narrow stripes I used a thin brush and a liner. Note that the check goes into the gaps between the fruit only up to a point and not right into the middle.

Above The striped border on this fresh cloth was painted with a sponge roller, a thin brush and some liner. The daisies in the centre were negative stencils, around which the blue background was sponge painted. Details were added to the daisies by using positive stencils. A sheer organza tea-net with daisies stencilled in opaque white was made to match (see photo on page 11).

Right This is a great way to do quick checks, with no white showing. I sponged the entire piece of seed cloth with watered-down blue paint to retain the texture of the seed cloth. Once this had dried, I used wide tape to mask out a border. Using a narrow roller, I made a check grid in pale green and then added thinner, darker stripes with a liner. This bled into the fabric in places, but as it was 'evenly uneven', it added to the effect. The tape was removed and leaves added in the two greens with a brushstroke for each. Black liner added the final outlines and spirals. The matching tablecloth was given the same check treatment, with the leaf pattern repeated in the centre square.

Resists have been used for centuries to decorate fabrics. Batik, the most common form of wax resist and probably the best-known resist art form, has its roots in the east. There are many books available on this specialised art form.

Closer to home there is a wealth of fabric designs throughout Africa in which other methods of resist are used, most notably the 'mud cloths' of Mali where mud is used to create striking black and white geometric patterns, and the 'Sadsa cloths' from Zimbabwe with mainly scenes of village life on dark backgrounds, painted in opaque paint.

Resists are used to block out areas of fabric, keeping them free from paint. We have outlined various ways to create effects with the resist technique. The most common method involves outlining patterns or motifs with paste and, once these outlines are dry, filling the areas between the outlines with fabric paint. The paste boundary prevents the paint from spreading. A feature of this technique is that the outlines retain the original cloth colour. This is very striking if used on dark fabric and painted with opaque paints.

A different form of resist is to use starch for a crackled background which can be either left as is, or decorated further.

FLOUR AND WATER PASTE

The most common and easily accessible resist medium used is a flour and water mixture: one part water to 1½ parts flour, with the consistency of thick white-sauce. This mixture can be kept in the fridge overnight so you can spread out working on a project over two days. Laundry starch or cornflour pastes are also used for resists, but when used for a crackled effect, the cracks are much finer.

Pour starch into a bottle with a nozzle to form lines – tomato sauce bottles, perm bottles, or craft bottles are ideal. The softer the bottle the easier the application becomes. For backgrounds, apply the paste with a spatula, scraper, spoon, paintbrush or your hands.

CORNFLOUR PASTE

For finer cracks, make a paste with cold water and 2 tablespoons of cornflour or laundry starch. Add 1 cup boiling water and stir thoroughly. Allow to cool. You may need to cook the mixture for 30 seconds or more in the microwave until clearish. Stir well and allow to cool. Skim off skin and use. The starch can be used hot, but take care not to burn yourself. If children will be working with the mixture it must be left to cool. Apply to fabric, crackle when dry and rub paint into cracks.

Hints

- If you make mistakes when outlining a design with paste, leave to dry and then remove the spot. Never try and wash it out while wet. You'll end up redoing the entire design.
- If you find it hard to crack a cloth covered in paste, bend or pull it over something sturdy such as the back of wooden chair or the edge of a table to loosen it. Ironing the back also helps.
- The fineness of cracks will depend on how thickly the starch has been applied: the thicker the starch the heavier and coarser the cracks.
- If you use opaque colours (including white), in a design, crackle after painting as the opaques will block out the crackle lines.
- When using crackle, if you are not going to cover the entire cloth with colour, it is best to use cream or beige fabric – white fabric looks too new and spoils the antique effect.

A medley of starch resists and designs. The cloth is a simple, leafy line-design which has been sponged in a pale blue with purple shading. The three cushions are good examples of painting on a crackled background. The two lighthouses were painted on fine cracks done with a cornflour mixture and the olives on coarser cracks done with flour. Painting on a crackled background works best in various shades of the same hue, as is evident from these examples.

Starch resist

Starch resist is also called the pasta technique or the flour and water technique. It is important to stretch the fabric before applying the starch, as the starch shrinks when dry. This causes the fabric to crumple. A sticky board is ideal and this is the one time you may leave fabric on it to dry! It will not stick. If you don't have a sticky board or stretch frame, weight the edges of the fabric with piles of books or other heavy objects or tape it to your work surface.

You will need

Fabric
Design enlarged to size (see page 148)
Blue tailor's pen – do not use pencil as this will show when you remove the starch lines
Sticky board or stretch frame
Flour and water paste (see page 92) in bottle with nozzle
Paint
Sponge
Paintbrush
Rounded butter knife

1 Trace the design onto the fabric with a blue tailor's pen. Using the bottle with a nozzle, trace the design with the paste in a continuous unbroken line. This should look like soft, cooked spaghetti lying on the fabric surface – the paste should 'sit' on top of the fabric and not be pushed in.

2 The starched fabric should now be left to dry flat, after which you can chip off any spots that shouldn't be there. A lighter mark will remain. Do not leave unpainted starch around for too long, as your average mouse finds it quite delicious and will move house for this free food supply.

3 Apply paint to the entire cloth working right up to the starch lines and into the corners that have been created by the starch. Take care not to chip off the starch lines. You can use a sponge, sea sponge, or brush to paint in your design, depending on the effect you wish to create.

4 If you wish, add shadows using a paintbrush.

5 When the paint is dry, remove the paste lines by lifting them off with a rounded butter knife. Never use a sharp knife – it is too easy to rip your

FILLING IN AND CRACKLING A MOTIF

For an interesting variation, fill in larger areas of your design and crackle these instead of painting the design over a crackled background. Use laundry starch or cornflour for finer cracks.

1 Trace the design onto the fabric with a blue tailor's pen. Using a bottle with a nozzle, trace the design with the paste in a continuous unbroken line.
2 Fill in solid areas of the design by covering them with starch, using a brush or small spatula. Take care not to spoil your outline and wash the brush immediately after use.
3 When the paste is dry, crack it by crumpling or rolling, so that small cracks appear all over. Apply paint to the entire cloth, filling the cracks on the design, as well as the uncrackled background.
4 To remove the dried paste, follow steps 6 and 7 on page 97.

fabric. You can also pick the starch off with your fingers. Try not to get it under your nails – it hurts. If the starch sticks, pull the fabric over the edge of a table to loosen it.

6 Heat set and wash out excess paste before using the fabric.

Crackled background

Apart from outlining, you can also use starch to crackle different areas. If you use sun or liquid paint over this, it seeps in underneath the starch and creates interesting effects of its own. Remember to stretch the fabric before applying the starch and to leave it like that to dry.

You will need

Fabric
Sticky board or stretch frame
Flour and water mixture
Spatula or scraper
Paint
Sponge or paintbrush
Rounded butter knife
Design enlarged to size (optional)
Blue tailor's pen
Paint as dictated by your design

1 Smear the paste over the desired area. This can either be over an entire background, around a motif or just fill the motif.

2 As a variation on a plain crackled background, scratch a pattern into the wet starch to create an interesting effect. Leave to dry on the sticky board.

3 When the paste is dry, crack it by crumpling or rolling, so that small cracks appear all over. You can check where you are by holding the fabric up to the light.

4 Apply paint all over the dry paste with a sponge or brush, making sure it penetrates into the cracks.

5 Check the back of the cloth again, to make sure the paint has penetrated. Don't push it in too hard, as the paint will bleed. Leave to dry.

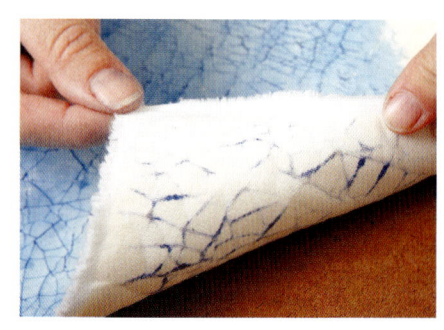

DIFFERENT CRACKS FROM DIFFERENT PASTE

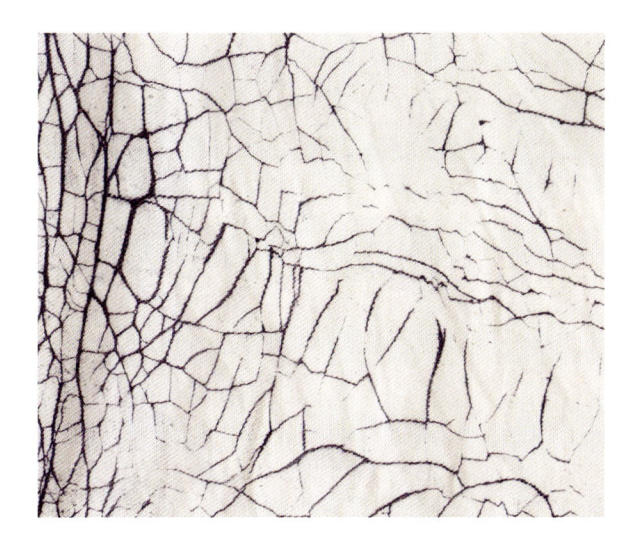

The larger cracks that result from a flour and water paste.

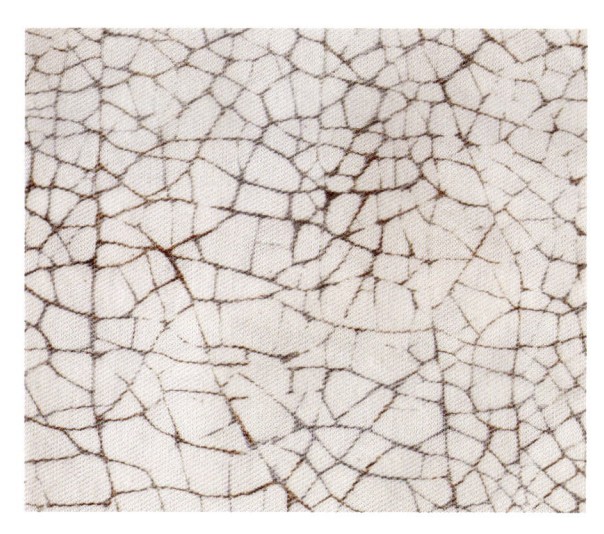

A mixture of wallpaper paste into flour paste resulted in these regular cracks.

Scratching a pattern in the wet starch will give the effect shown here.

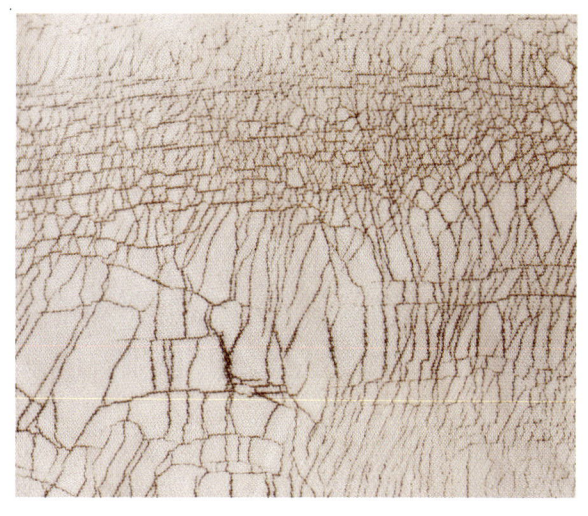

Laundry starch results in the finest cracks, as can be seen above.

6 Iron the back of the cloth thoroughly before soaking it in water for about 15 minutes. Lift the wet paste with a butter knife. This is like lifting thick porridge, so have a plastic bag ready in which to put it. Rinse the fabric a few times, but don't rub it, as it has not yet been properly heat set.

7 After heat setting, any excess paste can be washed out. You can now trace and paint a design over the crackled background. Use transparent paint so that you can see the cracks through it. This gives a worn appearance.

Resist combination

Having quite a penchant for African patterns and designs, I decided to use the Ghanaian Adinkra symbols as resist designs for a comforter. These symbols all have specific meanings which we have included with the templates at the back (see pages 148–149). The Ghanaian fabrics are usually patterned with stamps made from sections of calabashes.

Although large, this quilt was actually quite simple to paint as it consists of squares and lengths of fabric painted separately. I used several resist techniques, all done with the flour and water paste: outlining with a liner bottle; crackling larger areas, filling in and crackling a motif; and scratching into the wet starch to create lines within the crackled background. The cushions include starching on a dark fabric and sun painting over starched motifs.

You will need

- White, beige and navy fabric cut into squares and strips to make up a quilt front
- Flour and water paste (see page 92) in a bottle with a nozzle
- Designs enlarged to size (see pages 148–149)
- Blue tailor's pen
- Sticky board
- Paint: transparent navy, four shades of blue
- Sponge
- Paintbrush
- Rounded butter knife
- Materials to sew a quilt

1 Work out your comforter layout and place the designs.

2 For sections with outlined designs, trace the relevant designs onto the squares, using a blue tailor's pen. Outline each design with the flour and water paste and allow to dry completely while keeping the fabric flat. Solid sections of designs can also be starched. It is easiest to outline first with the liner bottle and to fill in the section to be starched with a paintbrush or other applicator. Wash the brush immediately after use.

3 Sponge over in pale blue. Shade in where necessary with a darker blue, using a sponge or brush.

4 When the paint is dry, remove the paste lines by lifting them off with a rounded butter knife. If the starch sticks, pull the fabric over the edge of a table to loosen it.

5 Heat set and wash out excess paste before using the fabric.

6 For sections with a crackled background, pour starch paste onto the fabric and smooth it out with an applicator. Dry flat – this takes a while.

7 Crack by rolling or crumpling and coat with colour making sure the paint penetrates the cracks – you can check this at the back or by holding the fabric up to the light.

8 Leave to dry, then iron the back of the cloth thoroughly before soaking the cloth in water for about 15 minutes. Lift the wet paste with a butter knife and rinse the fabric a few times. Don't rub it though, as it has not yet been properly heat set.

9 After heat setting, any excess paste can be washed out. You can now trace and paint a design over the crackled background. Use transparent paint so that you can see the cracks through it. This gives a worn appearance.

10 Make up the comforter according to your layout.

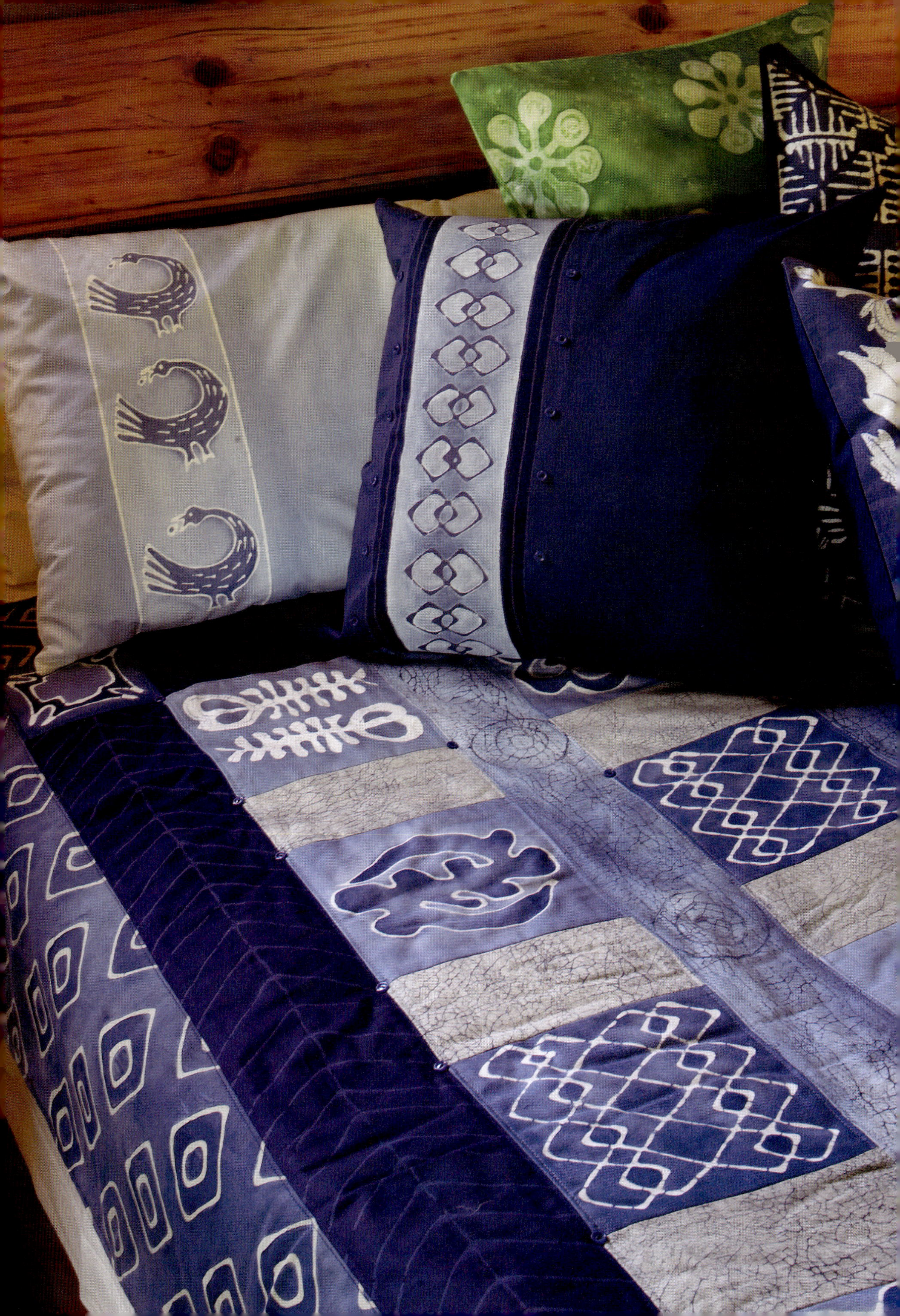

Above These designs both have outlines of starch resist, and the rust-coloured cloth has solid, crackled areas as well. The top cloth was a simple outline on black fabric, which was filled in with metallic paint. Different shades of gold, silver and copper were obtained by using paint from different manufacturers. The yellow fabric used for the rust-coloured cloth was dry brushed all over with black after the starch was applied and cracked. Once the black paint was dry, the cloth was sponged all over with ochre. While this was still wet, I sponged darker red and rust shading in the areas which I wanted to stand out. I then sponged chocolate brown shading around these areas.

Left For the seat cover starch resist was used with a Mali 'mud cloth' pattern on cream fabric, over-painted with black and taupe The labyrinth cushion on the left was painted with opaque and pearl paints, shading darker to the centre, with the original black cloth showing the starch resist pattern. The striped cushion with spiral motifs was lightly dragged with black over orange and taupe bands. Spirals and lines were then scraped with a wooden clothes peg into the wet paint. Scribbling and smudging with black and gold liners on bought fabric turned the topmost cushion into an eye-catching, yet quick and easy fabric-painting project. In the foreground you see the result of solid starch resist crackle on black fabric.

Left The starch lines on this duvet cover had to be applied in two sessions as it is a king-size cover and I didn't have enough space to lay it out flat. The design is based on a series of Adinkra symbols which were also used in the quilt project. Here the starch treatment and paint colours result in an earthy, more traditional African feel, than the contemporary blue tones of the quilt. The *Kra Pa* symbol was chosen for the cushion cover as it means good fortune. This was dry brushed onto Mopane worm silk and then roughly outlined with black and gold liners. Serendipity led to finding the matching raffia fringing at an obscure junk shop!

Right We are very blessed to live in a suburb with large open areas and look out onto a wide green-belt teeming with guinea fowl. They are quite used to the neighbourhood cats, and have been known to keep the odd 'hostage' stuck up a tree for some time. They inspired this bedcover and matching cushions, with a border of starch resist, shaded in tones of pale ochre, tan, rust and grey with geometric details scratched in with the back of a brush. The guineas themselves were shaded in reds, blue greys and charcoal with the spots on the bodies made with opaque white liner. You don't see the cat? He's probably still up the tree!

stencilling

A stencil is a simple shape punched out of card or plastic and is a quick method of repeating a design. Stencils come in a wide range of sizes and motifs and are readily available.

Stencils can be positive or negative. A positive stencil is where the actual motif has been cut away, in other words the cut-outs (windows) form the design to be used. The thin areas separating these windows are called bridges, and attach the inner portions of the design so that they are held in place. A single stencil has the complete design on one sheet, and is usually painted in one colour.

More complex designs may need multiple stencils, one sheet for each colour or shade. A multiple stencil is laid onto the fabric one sheet after the other so that the image is built up.

A negative stencil is a solid shape, the motif itself forming a mask or block out with the area around it being painted. This is usually a simple shape or design, for example a heart or an entire flower. Negative stencilling is particularly useful when painting a flat, smooth background.

Stencils are often applied over a painted or decorated background.

GUIDELINES FOR SUCCESSFUL STENCILLING

- Use a stencil brush, sponge, sea sponge, scrunched up plastic bag, bubble wrap or any similar applicator to apply the paint through the stencil windows. A stencil brush is much better than an ordinary paintbrush as it is round and softer with cut off bristles and gives a better finish.
- Always load your applicator sparingly. If too much paint is applied, it is likely to seep under the edges of the stencil.
- Apply the paint by dabbing it down rather than using normal brushstrokes which may distort the template. Dabbing the paint onto the fabric will produce a lightly speckled or textured effect.
- You can also use a circular motion from the outer edges of the stencil to the centre, building up the colour as you go. Add more colour to create shading. Use different shades of the same colour to create lighter and darker areas. Adding other colours can also create nice shaded effects.
- Never stencil with a damp or wet sponge or brush, as it will cause the edges of the design to blur.
- When you use multiple stencils it is often best to leave the first elements of your design to dry before applying the next stencil. This prevents the painted elements from smudging.
- Paint your stencil with pressure sensitive adhesive (stencil glue) and allow to dry. This allows the back of the stencil to stick to the fabric, so that the stencil doesn't move. Protect the glued surface with a cut open, unprinted plastic shopping bag when the stencil is not in use.

Making your own stencils

Making your own stencils offers more possibilities than using simple bought ones. You can use any of the simple designs included in the templates to make your own stencils. And instead of buying PVC or acetate, use an old X-ray cleaned in a strong bleach solution.

You will need

Design enlarged to size (see design page 158–159) on a piece of paper
Clear PVC, acetate or X-ray
Craft knife
Cutting board

1 Tape PVC over your design and trace with a black marker. Make sure there is quite a large border of PVC around the design, otherwise you will have a problem with overflow when using the stencil.

2 Cut the windows out with a sharp craft knife or scalpel, making sure you include enough bridges between the windows to hold the design together. Use a cutting board, as a sharp craft knife will damage your work surface.

3 If your stencil is to be multi-layered, use separate sheets of PVC for each colour, taking care to include registration marks on each sheet to ensure accurate positioning when you use the stencil.

Stencilling this cushion and bolster cover is described on page 105. Templates for both multi-layered rose designs are on pages 158 and 159. The roses and leaves on the folded tablecloth were monoprinted on a dry-brushed background with stencilled lettering.

techniques

Simple stencilling

You will need

Prepared simple stencil (see design page 156)
Heavy-weight cotton fabric
Small sponge or stencil brush
Chalk or purple tailor's pen
Black fabric paint
Extender
Materials to finish skirt

Stencil traditional Xhosa designs in black on traditional isikaka or a heavy-weight cream fabric and make a wrap-around skirt finished with rows of interesting braiding.

1 Sew the basic skirt. Plan the design repeat across the bottom border of the skirt. Mark in the repeat positions with chalk or purple tailor's pen.

2 Stencil the design repeatedly across the border using the sponge or stencil brush and various shades of black paint as in the photograph.

3 Allow paint to dry completely and heat set by ironing. Stitch braiding on either side of the design for the distinctive traditional look. You can substitute paint for braid by laying masking tape strips around the border and painting between them to create parallel lines.

VARIATION

This simple stencil is a silhouette. It can be coloured in freehand or make a colour-fill stencil with windows specially cut to fit exactly over the simple stencil design. Dab coloured paint in a repeat pattern through this stencil to fill in the black line-design making it look as like a screen-print.

Multi-layered roses

Stencilling on a painted background produces exciting results combining different textural effects with a stencilled motif. Multi-layered stencils look more three-dimensional than the simple stencils.

The designs for these stencils were created from photographs on a computer. I did the colour separations by manipulating the light/brightness settings and settled on four degrees of separation. The more separations used, the more realistic the stencilled motif.

You will need

Fabric for cushion cover/bolster
Prepared multi-layered stencil (see design page 158–159)
Sponges
Paint: transparent burgundy, four shades of pink
Extender
Materials to make up cushion cover/bolster

1 Cloud the fabric as described on page 117. Use extender or a really pale colour for the initial layer and keep the background light, as the rose will be stencilled on top. For a contrasting background, use the solid rose shape as a block out (negative stencil). For multiple roses, cut more negative shapes as accurately as possible. Place them in position and sponge in the darker background. Leave to dry completely, as the stencil will not stick to wet paint.

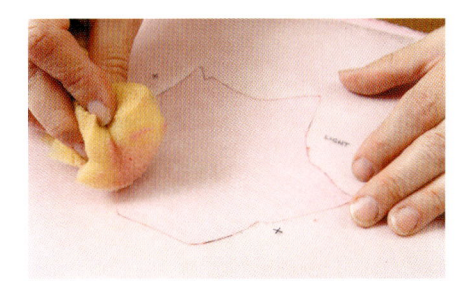

2 Place the first rose stencil in position and sponge in the lightest pink. This forms a solid base for the rest of the rose. Load the sponge sparingly as too much paint will cause bleeding under the edges of the stencil, spoiling the effect. Leave the stencil in place.

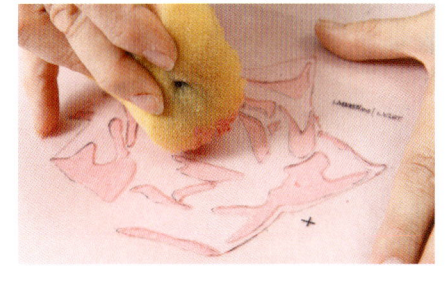

3 Place the second stencil over the first, matching the registration marks. Use masking tape to keep it in place if necessary. Sponge in the next shade.

4 Repeat the process with the rest of the stencils, sponging in the relevant rose shades. Allow to dry, heat set and make up a cushion and a bolster.

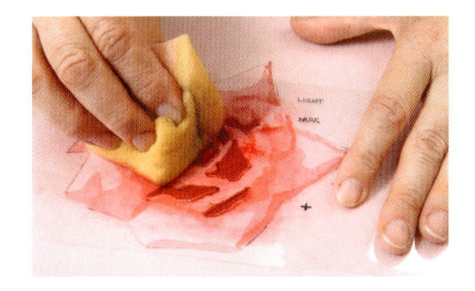

Negative shadow-technique

Negative stencilling can be combined with a shadow technique to create a really interesting effect. By lifting and replacing a single stencil shape all over your cloth and working around it with a sponge, a shadow effect is created. This technique works especially well with flower and leaf motifs, although any shape will do as long as it is a single negative stencil. Do not pre-glue these 'moving' stencils.

You will need

Fabric for window covers
Prepared negative stencil (see design on page 153)
Sticky board
Paint: transparent beige, dark beige, red, orange, magenta, pale grey-green
Liner: transparent red
Extender
Sponges
Paintbrush
Materials to make up window covers

1 Lay the fabric on a sticky board and sponge with beige paint all over.

2 Using two shades of red at a time, sponge oval shapes, here and there. I did this only three times on each of the panels. Change to different tones, (including orange and magenta) as you go, creating a blotchy, uneven effect.

3   While the paint is still wet, place the flower stencil on an oval and sponge dark beige around the shape. Work the dark colour into the lighter background tone, taking care not to make a ring around the flower, but rather a soft, pinky shadow.

4   To create a background of shadow poppies, repeat this, shading all over in beige only, overlapping the flowers as you go. Do not shade the area where two shapes intersect, as you will end up with a double shape that will make no sense. The flower that is shaded second should look as if it is peeping out from behind the first. Wipe the stencil clean between repeats.

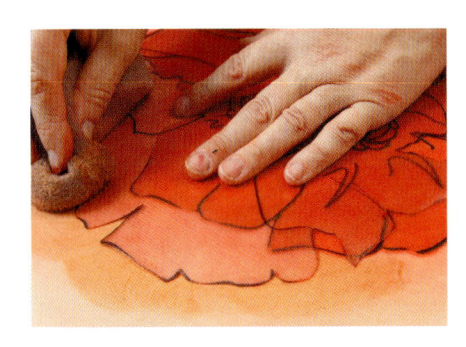

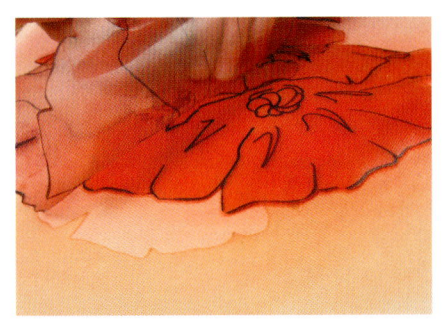

5   Scratch in the flower details with the back of a paintbrush while the paint is still wet.

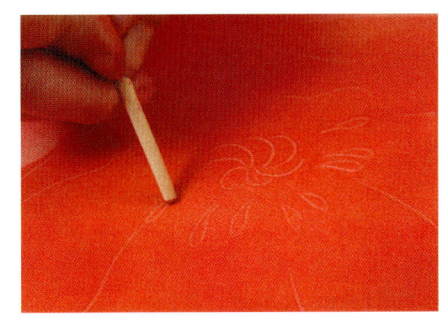

6   Once the paint is dry, add a darker colour to the red flowers for further shading, if necessary. The stems can be filled in lightly towards the top with a pale grey green, using a brush.

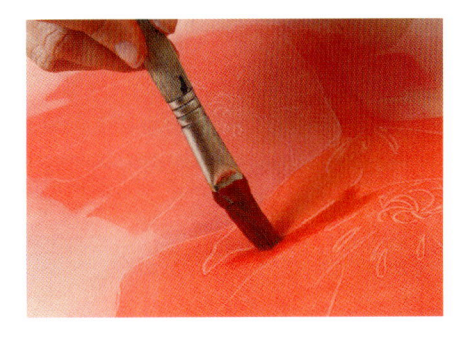

7   Red liner is finally added to emphasize detail on the poppies.

8   Allow to dry thoroughly, heat set and make up window covers. For a wider window, paint a field of poppies instead of long-stemmed flowers.

African pot variation

The stencilling technique used on the pot and the painted frame is great if you want a slightly more realistic effect than when you are using a conventional stencil with bridges. The leaves and orchids were painted and shaded over a traced design. I used a beautiful piece of grey Thai silk which I had left from another project I did years ago, so I used opaque white to help with the shading of the flowers.

You will need

Fabric
Design enlarged to size (see page 146)
Glued PVC or acetate for stencil
Craft knife
Masking tape
Paint: transparent taupe, charcoal, magenta, pink, yellow, green; opaque white
Extender
Sponge
Paintbrushes

1 Trace the pot shape onto the PVC, including the top rim lines and the bottom line of the pattern. On a separate piece of PVC trace the outline of the leaves – not the detail. Cut these out carefully – you need both negative and positive stencils of the pot and the negative stencil of the leaves. Cut along the rim lines and bottom pattern line of the negative pot stencil.

2 Place the positive stencil of the pot on the fabric with the leaves in position at the top. Carefully fill in the pot with a sponge, using dark taupe – leave a light area in the middle for a highlight.

3 Shade around the edges of the entire pot with charcoal.

4 Place the negative middle section of the pot inside the positive stencil and shade with charcoal along the bottom edge. Place the thin top strip of the pot in position, underneath the rim. Shade with charcoal on either side.

5 Leave the pot as is or add the decorative detail by painting, scratching or further stencilling. I used charcoal paint over a hand-cut stencil.

6 Trace the leaves and flowers with a pencil and paint in, referring to the photograph for realistic shading. Allow to dry thoroughly.

7 Mark along the inside of the painted frame with masking tape. Mix magenta and taupe into extender, making a dirty pink. Sponge in the frame.

8 Shade along the outside edge of the frame, along the top and down the left side with charcoal. Repeat shading along the inside edge of the frame down the right side and along the bottom (use the photograph as a guide). Place a piece of scrap paper across one corner at a time, shading with charcoal as follows: top left: towards centre; top right: downwards and both bottom corners towards the centre. Leave to dry.

9 I added further dimension by masking off thin stripes within the frame, and shading with charcoal. Neaten the corners by lifting the tape crossover point gently and trimming to square.

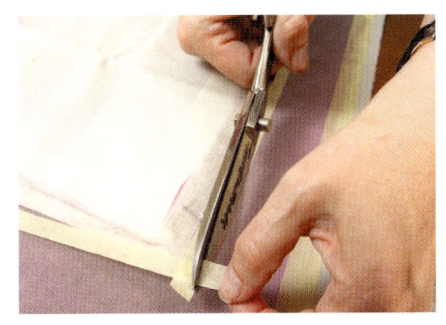

10 Finish with a dry-brush shadow under the pot.

Right As large block-out stencils of various sizes of nasturtiums were used for this cloth, the painting surface had to be the size of the cloth or larger. The background was covered in a pale yellow and then dragged over with red and purple together, without mixing them on the palette first. The leaves and veins were scratched in, but I found the effect rather stark, so I brushed over the entire background lightly with the same wide brush I'd just used. This softened the effect and the leaves no longer jumped out. When the background was dry I lifted the negative stencils and used a positive stencil to fill in the nasturtium details in various shades of yellow and orange, shading slightly in red. Some details were scratched out with the back of a brush.

Left What fun it was painting this cloth! The drawings of cups, sugar bowls and pots were done by looking at the item and not the paper, resulting in skew and interesting shapes. These were then traced onto the cloth in black pen. The cloth was sponged with yellow. I then painted blocks of colour over the images in red, purple, magenta or orange while the yellow was wet. (This could also be done over dry yellow) While these blocks of colour were wet, various shaped stamps (blocks, spirals, diamonds and so on) were impressed and then used to stamp on elsewhere. The words (cappuccino, coffee, café, espresso) were enlarged on the computer and stencils cut out of plastic. When all the painted areas were dry, they were stencilled into the open areas to add interest and texture.

Right Feeling that the traditional colours of red and green have become a little jaded, I decided to do something cooler for Christmas. I used loads of techniques: stencils were placed in position to block out the dove shapes, so that they would remain white. The background was then clouded with blue and purple, and while it was wet, star shapes were stamped off. I used a wide brush and made a scalloped border, also in blue and purple, picking up some of each colour at the same time. When the paint was dry I added 'curl' stencils and the words *Joyeaux Noël* in a medium blue. The snowflakes were added with opaque white – yes, they're stencils, as are the stars, added in silver. Finally, the dove stencils were removed and details added with navy and silver liner, which was also added to the border.

Left Block-out stencils were used for the water lilies and the leaf attached to them. The background of blue, turquoise, teal green and lime was sponged over the block outs in streaks, almost creating stripes. Using three different sized leaves for the shadow stencilling, the background was then shaded with either turquoise or green, depending on where the leaves were placed. If the background was teal, green was used for shading and if it was blue or turquoise, dark turquoise was used. Once the leafy area was dry, the water lilies were shaded, using opaque white and magenta with yellow in the centres.

stencilling gallery

The placemat was stencilled with the running buck design using both the positive and negative cut outs. The mat was first sponged unevenly with peach paint. While still wet the negative stencils were placed in position and darker rust paint rubbed over them to create shadows which show up the lighter buck running in the foreground. The negative stencils were left in place and overlaid by positive stencils for a darker row of different running buck to be dabbed through it. The darker buck were positioned to show 'behind' the front runners.

The table-runner design used only the legs of the same buck stencils to create a patterned border using the same light and dark negative and positive stencil rubbing/dabbing technique. The border edge was first masked out with a rectangular piece of paper. These are very quick and effective stencils to use – cutting them takes quite a while though and lots of patience.

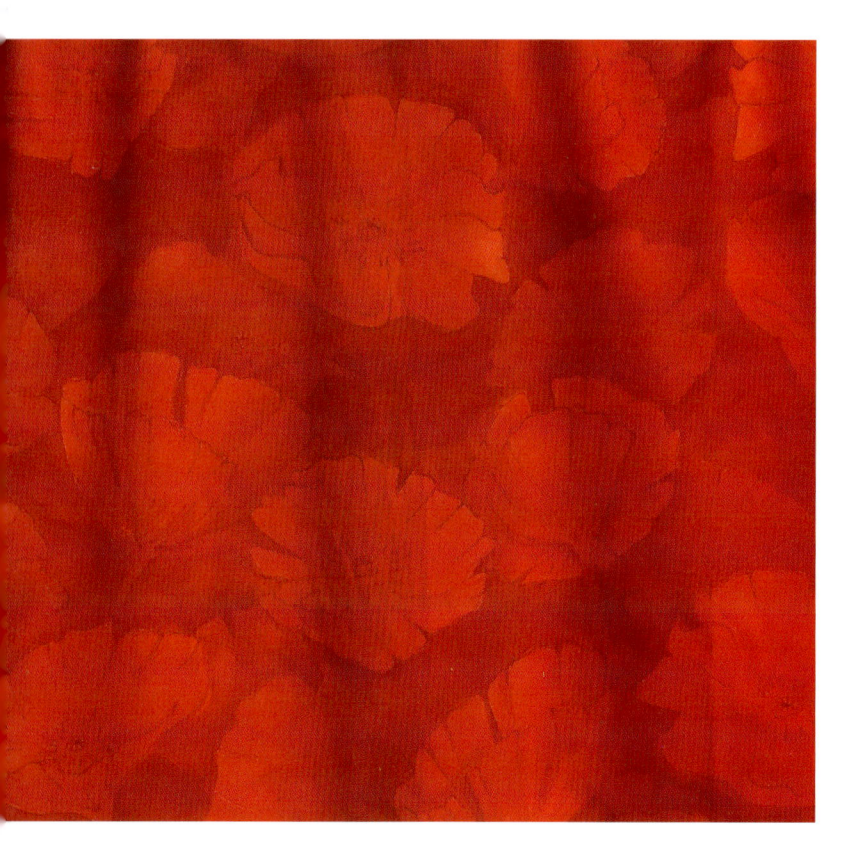

As an alternative to the pale poppies on tall stems I painted this field of poppies using strong reds. The background was first sponged randomly with magenta, red, brick red and orange. Using large negative stencils I shadow-painted around the shapes with burgundy, while the first layer of paint was still wet, detail was added with a dark red liner. When dry, I also added a little shading in brick red to the centre of the flowers to add depth.

LEFT Inspired by African skies and dust clouds we used a variety of stencilling techniques to bring these herds of elephant onto this combination of cushions. Brown tones have resulted from using the complementary colours of orange and purple, in various tints and shades. While the elephants in the background are simple silhouettes, texture was added to the elephants in the foreground in the front cushion by bagging over positive stencils with crumpled paper. Shading was added for definition once the paint was dry.

RIGHT An autumn-leaf deign was used to disguise garden grime on the tatty insoles of my gardening clogs. This led to designing and painting an exclusive matching apron! I used negative leaf stencils for the inside and back of the apron – I traced actual leaves for accurate shapes. The front pockets were stencilled with positive leaf images on a plain background.

The entire apron was then coated with a waterproofing agent.

stencilling gallery

stamp & print

Stamping and printing are great ways of reproducing the same motif many times without redrawing and painting it each time. These techniques are most effective when applied over a painted background.

Bought stamps, usually made from rubber, foam rubber or sponge, are the easiest to use. The larger, bold stamps are best suited to fabric painting, as finely detailed images will generally not print too clearly on fabric. Fabric paint will stain the stamps, but don't use bleach to clean them as this will cause the rubber to perish and they will become sticky. Be careful when cleaning wood-backed stamps or carved wooden stamps. Just wipe them clean with a damp sponge immediately after use. Don't soak them in water – they will warp and split.

Stamps can be made from just about anything, from a piece of cardboard to a calabash, like the Adinkra stamps from Ghana, as long as the stamping surface is level. Try some of these ideas, each of which will give its own effect, so experiment to your heart's content:

- Found objects such as corks, cork tiles, vinyl, bottle tops, screws, corrugated cardboard, cut-outs from textured punnets, or natural objects such as feathers and leaves.
- Hard vegetables and fruit are ideal when halved. You can either use them for their natural shape, or carve a design into the surface, (most effective with a potato). Leave the halved vegetable or fruit for at least 30 minutes to dry, flat side down on absorbent paper, otherwise the moisture affects the paint and causes it to bleed when the print is made.
- Sponge cleaning-cloth is great. Either cut out a shape, glue it to board and use this as a stamp, or roll the cloth to make a 'curly whirly'. To make a culry whirly, cut two strips of cloth, one narrower than the other; roll the narrower of the two inside the wider strip. When completely rolled up, secure with masking tape. You can also simply use the edge as a straight line or bend it for a U or a V shape.
- Rubber is easily cut with a cutting knife or scalpel – recycle old slip slops, old hot-water bottles, erasers, old shoe soling, and so on.
- Lino is ideal for carved stamps and is available from craft shops.
- Polystyrene and high-density foam are also great materials into which to carve an image. Use a ballpoint pen for engraving onto high-density foam.

Stamping basics

Making a stamp pad
You can make your own stamp pad with a small sheet of thick plastic and a thin piece of sponge. Glue the sponge onto the plastic on either or both sides. To use, paint the stamp with the colours you wish to use – this can be multicoloured for interesting variations on coloured backgrounds. Print the stamp onto the pad. Load the pad with more colour in the areas you have stamped. When you have done this, pick up the colour with the stamp as you would with an office stamp and pad. This is easier than painting onto the stamp each time.

Inking the stamp
There are a number of ways, depending on the object and type of paint you are using. Stamp pads can be inked with permanent drawing inks, liquid pigment dyes, or emulsion fabric paints. Each gives its own effect. Whichever method or medium you use, ensure that the stamp is evenly coated, but do not use too much paint or ink, or the result will be blurry.

- Use a soft sponge or a paintbrush to dab colour evenly onto the stamp surface, or use a stamp pad as described above.
- Coat a small foam roller with paint and roll this evenly over the stamp a few times.
- Paint a thin coat of paint onto a flat polystyrene tray. Stamp the clean stamp onto this a few times.
- Fine items such as leaves and feathers are impressed veined side down, into pre-painted surfaces such as plastic or glass or a flat polystyrene tray before printing.

Making a print
After inking your stamp with an even a layer of paint, place it onto your fabric and press down, rocking gently. Firm, even pressure is required for an even print. Don't press down hard with a few fingers, especially when using sponges, as your fingertips will make darker marks. Rather press with a piece of board or the heel of your hand.

When stamping off (removing paint from the painted surface for negative images), always use clean, dry stamps.

Printing with a feather

Stamping or printing with natural found objects is easy and effective, as long as the surface is relatively flat. A great favourite of mine is to use a feather – any dam is a great source, or the beach, if you're lucky enough to live at the coast. A medium to small feather will work better than a very large one, as the quill becomes too thick for printing. I used clouding for the background of this bag as it works so well with the feather. You would print with a leaf in exactly the same way.

You will need

Fabric for laundry bag
Sponge
Large brush
Paint: transparent, pale blue, periwinkle blue, sky blue, teal green, navy
Extender
Paintbrush or sponge roller
Plastic sheet
Feather(s)
Lots of waste paper
Materials to make laundry bag

1 Cover the fabric in a very pale colour – a little of the main background colour mixed with extender will work. While the cloth is wet, using the main colour of choice and a big brush, cross-hatch across the cloth. It is fine if it ends up darker in some places.

2 While still wet, use a sponge in a circular motion, to blend the paint, creating a soft, cloudy effect. More than one colour can be used. I used periwinkle blue, sky blue and teal green.

3 Continue with the cross hatching/blending until you are happy with the result. Don't use too many colours as you may end up with a gloomy rain cloud. Allow to dry.

4 Apply the navy paint as evenly as possible to the piece of plastic using a brush or roller, and place the feather onto the painted plastic.

5 Put a piece of paper over of the feather and rub gently. This will ensure that the feather becomes completely coated with paint.

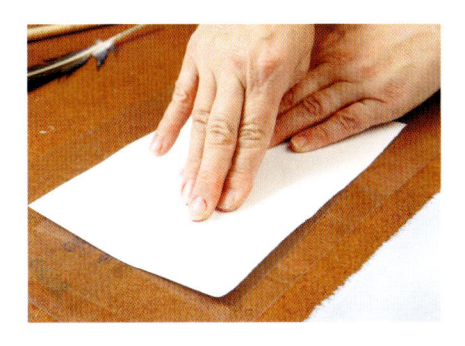

6 Remove the paper, carefully lift the feather off the plastic and place it paint side down onto the fabric.

7 Place a clean sheet of paper over the feather and rub, so transferring the paint to the fabric.

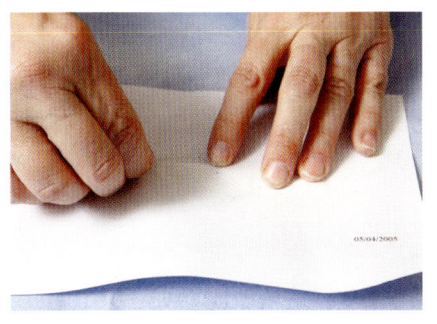

8 Repeat as many times as you like. The feather will eventually become clogged with paint and should then be replaced with a fresh one.

9 Allow to dry thoroughly, heat set and make the laundry bag.

Bought stamps

You will need

White cotton fabric
Sponges
Paint: transparent yellow, orange, magenta, black
Extender
Various bug stamps
Plastic fork
Denim and materials for a backpack

Here's a great idea to keep a bug collector happy. Get him involved in making a stamped pocket, closing flap and shoulder-strap pads for a backpack. Remember, we warned you that this book is not about sewing – you'll have to find your own backpack pattern! I used black bull denim for the bag, and white cotton for the fabric-painted sections.

1 Sponge the white cotton fabric with extender. Work it in well so that the cloth is not slick and wet.

2 Sponge the paints across the cloth, in bands, blending and dragging them so that they form a bright harmony or transition of colour (see dragging, page 67).

3 While the paint is still wet, impress the various stamps in a few rows across the fabric, lifting off the colour (stamping off).

4 Use the fork to draw wavy patterns into the paint between the rows of stamped-off bugs. Allow to dry well.

5 Stamp more bugs onto the dried background between the stamped-off images, using black or a dark colour. Allow to dry thoroughly.

6 Heat set, cut the fabric to suit your pattern and sew the bag.

Home-made stamps

I made this simple duffel bag from a rectangle of fabric, stamped with homemade lizard and geometric stamps, joined around a circular denim base. Bought stamps will work as well.

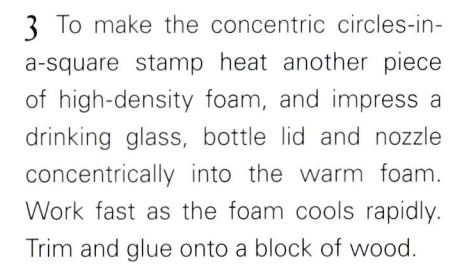

You will need

Fabric
Potato
Design enlarged to size (see page 146)
High density foam (cut up an old mouse-pad)
Craft knife
Wood blocks
White wood-flue
Drinking glass, bottle lid and nozzle
Sponge roller
Paint: transparent denim blue in various shades
Extender
Materials to make duffel bag

1 Cut a potato in half, with a large flat knife, so that the cut surfaces are absolutely flat to ensure even printing. Place face down on absorbent paper. When dry, draw on a simple lizard and carve out carefully. This makes a lizard positive for printing.

2 Heat a piece of high density foam under the oven's element until it begins to expand. Quickly stamp the lizard into the warm foam, pressing down evenly for a few seconds. You now have a negative (recessed) image of your stamp. Trim the foam to the desired size and shape and glue onto a suitable sized block of wood.

3 To make the concentric circles-in-a-square stamp heat another piece of high-density foam, and impress a drinking glass, bottle lid and nozzle concentrically into the warm foam. Work fast as the foam cools rapidly. Trim and glue onto a block of wood.

4 Apply layers of extender and denim blue paint with a sponge roller for an interesting textured background for stamping and stamping off. Stamp off while the paint is wet, allow to dry and complete the stamping.

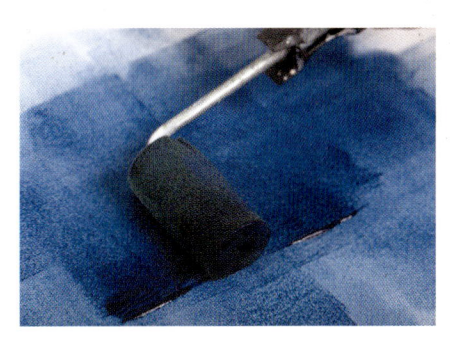

5 When you're happy with your stamping, allow to dry thoroughly, heat set and sew the duffel bag.

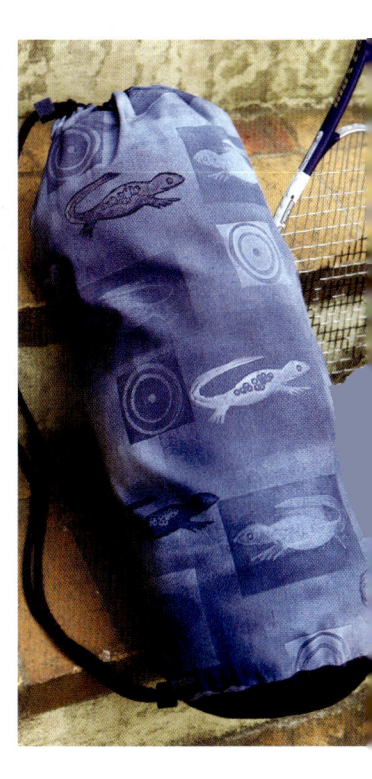

Stamping with sparkle

You will need

Black chiffon stole
Spiral stamps (I used home-made foam ones)
Paint: gold pearl paint with binder medium added
Sponge
Gold embossing powder or sparkle dust – the kind used for card making
Materials to finish stole

Give a plain chiffon evening shawl a beauty treatment by randomly stamping a simple design onto it. With these mostly synthetic fabrics you have to add binder medium/anti-bleed to your paint to make it colour fast. Your stole can be fringed with matching beads to make it look and feel really special.

1 Apply gold paint to a spiral stamp using the sponge. While the paint is still wet, puff a little sparkle dust or embossing powder onto it on the stamp.

2 Stamp onto chiffon, lift clear and blow off any excess gold dust. Repeat with stamps of different sizes.

3 Leave to dry thoroughly, heat set and finish to your taste.

Embossing

The velvet evening bag was decorated using the same spiral stamps, glitter glues and gold liner. For an extra special effect I embossed the stamped spirals on the velvet with a dry iron. You may need an extra pair of hands for this technique. Otherwise, take care not to burn yourself. I was alone and stuck the iron upside down in the vice on the garage workbench! This is a fabulous technique so do try it. Be careful not to press your stamp so deeply into the velvet pile that the stamp support surround also gets embossed, though. There's no cure for this except to repeat it and pretend that you intended the effect all along. And sewing velvet is awfully fiddly – lining it even worse. Pay someone to do it for you – it's worth it!

You will need

Design enlarged to size (see page 151)
Black velvet
Stamps
Iron
Paint: gold pearl paint mixed with binder medium
Gold embossing powder
Gold and silver glitter glue
Gold fabric liner
Materials to sew evening bag

1 Transfer the spiral design onto the fabric with chalk (see page 26), and lightly mark where you want the stamped, embossed spirals.

2 Load your stamp with pearl paint and dust with embossing powder.

3 Preheat the iron to the correct temperature for velvet (usually medium/synthetic). Hold the iron firmly upside down so that the sole-plate faces upwards and is level. Place the velvet pile side facing up (wrong side against the iron) onto the sole plate, and allow the velvet to heat up for about 10 seconds.

4 Press the loaded stamp firmly down onto the velvet on the iron and hold in position for about four seconds. Lift the stamp straight up, and voilà! You have stamped, embossed, painted, gilded and heat set your design in one go!

5 Complete the rest of the spiral design with gold and silver glitter glue and gold liner, incorporating the embossed spirals.

6 Sew an evening bag with the decorated velvet as a front or a fold-over flap. Decorate the shoulder strap with gold liner and silver glitter glue.

Hint

If you are using a steam iron, avoid pressing the stamp in the area of the vent holes.

Transfer-print collage

There are a number of ways to transfer printed images to fabric. These include liquid transfer mediums and iron-on transfer crayons which come with specific instructions for each brand and are available at craft shops. We chose a method especially suited to teenagers permanently plugged to PCs, namely printing colour pictures from scanned photos onto special iron-on inkjet transfer paper available at stationery shops. These transfers are bonded to fabric with an iron and are fully washable. They combine well with other fabric-paint techniques.

You will need

Pictures printed on iron-on transfer paper
T-shirt
T-shirt board
Iron
Paint: transparent magenta, purple
Extender
Brushes
Sponges
Stamps

1 Cut the pictures to size and lay out face down on a light box to determine collage positions. If you don't have a lightbox, do your lay-out face up, bearing in mind that everything must be reversed when ironed on.

2 Insert board into T-shirt and smooth down fabric. Don't use a sticky board as the heat from the iron will melt the glue into the T-shirt.

3 Mark picture positions very lightly on the T-shirt using a soft pencil. Take the pictures from the lay-out one at a time and iron into position on the fabric, following specific instructions supplied with the iron-on transfer paper.

4 Leave to cool down, then paint over and around the pictures with extender and colours to draw them together as one design. Use sponges, brushes and stamps to further embellish the collage.

5 Allow to dry thoroughly and heat set on the wrong side. To preserve your collage machine wash the T-shirt on a gentle cycle and do not iron directly on the printed area.

PHOTOCOPIED TRANSFERS

Ordinary black and white photocopied designs can be transferred to smooth, light-coloured fabric with lacquer thinners or acetone. The bolder the print the better the transfer.

1 Stretch fabric onto a work surface with masking tape. Do not use a sticky board, as lacquer thinners will dissolve the glue on the board and make a mess on your fabric.
2 Stick photocopy design in position with masking tape, face down on the fabric.
3 Soak a cotton-wool ball in thinners and rub firmly over the back of the photocopy, taking care not to shift the paper. Rub with the back of a spoon.
4 The design will print onto the fabric surface.
5 Leave thinners-soaked fabric to dry completely, and iron.
6 Paint over the design with extender to seal, or with fabric paints to colour and seal. Allow to dry and set properly.

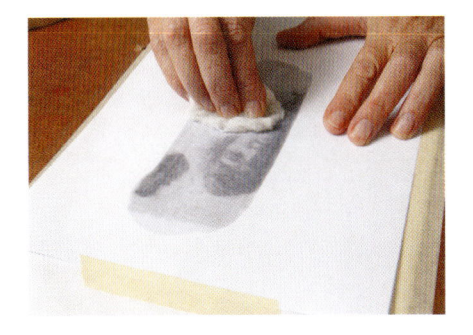

Hints
- If you are transferring lettering, photocopy them in reverse to print correctly.
- A great idea for a special gift for granny: transfer photos onto a tray-cloth or cushion cover – or if you are really ambitious, make a family heirloom quilt!

A simple screen-print

It seems strange to take a book on fabric painting one step into screen printing, but maybe this is the beginning of another journey and another book – (but not by us right now!). This very basic little screen uses fabric paint as printing ink and shows you how simple it is to screen-print your own labels. Use nail varnish instead of sanding sealer or shellac as for such a small screen there's no point in buying large quantities of block out or filler varnish.

We wanted to do the screen print so that we could print our own combined logos of the chameleon and the aardvark. We'll leave you guessing which is who … Remember the copyright story (see page 25)? Please design your own logo.

You will need

Design enlarged to size
Soft pencil
Small cheap wooden picture frame, glass and backing card removed
Scrap of glass organza or some other fine mesh fabric: enough to cover screen
Staple gun
Packaging tape
Phone card
Fine brush
Nail varnish
Fabric paint

1 Trace the design onto the mesh, using a soft pencil.

2 Place the frame over the mesh so that the design is inside the frame. Stretch and staple the mesh onto the outside of the frame – you may need extra hands to hold while stretching and stapling.

3 Turn the frame over and paint nail varnish over the screen, leaving the logo or design unpainted. This is a little fiddly so take care. Leave to dry thoroughly.

4 Frame the design or logo with packaging tape on both sides of the mesh. The packaging tape should extend from the design surround to the edges of the wooden frame. You now have a positive window through which you can screen print.

5 Position the screen on the fabric ready for printing. Hold it in place firmly while you print. Blob paint on one end of the screen and use a phone card as an applicator. It must be wide enough to cover the open design area of mesh.

6 Pull the paint firmly over the printing area with the card. You may need to pull twice to print through the mesh properly so practise on some scrap cloth until you get it right.

7 Remove the screen, allow the paint to dry thoroughly and heat set.

Monoprinted marbling

Follow these easy steps to magically transform your fabric into a swirl of marble. The marbled cotton was sewn into a reversible pocket onto a beach towel which folds neatly into the pocket. The addition of back-pack type shoulder bands makes this towel very practical.

Your will need

White fabric
Comb
Bleached X-ray or rigid plastic
Paint: transparent blue, magenta, turquoise
Extender
Credit card or squeegee
Large beach towel
Materials to sew towel bag

1 Mark off an area on the X-ray or rigid plastic, slightly bigger than the fabric you want to marble.

2 Place blobs of coloured fabric paint, interspersed with blobs of extender, onto that area.

3 Comb patterns into the paint with a variety of sticks, needles or combs. The shape, configuration and thickness of the items you use will affect the pattern created.

4 Lay the fabric over the paint and press down gently for the cloth to absorb the paint.

5 Lift and lay the fabric paint side up on a flat surface.

6 Scrape off all excess paint with a credit card or squeegee.

7 Allow to dry thoroughly, heat set and sew a towel bag.

Hint

Be warned: this is addictive and it uses a lot of paint and colours. But, you can mix up the left-overs to create a gunge base for mixing dark colours. I have what is known as 'The Gunge Bucket' in my studio and Monique has a 'Merry Mix' All leftovers get scraped into it. By adding pigment to the gunge, or mix, we have a permanent supply of brown or black paints.

Monoprinted children's art

You will need

Placemats
Simple designs
Print surface: large bleached X-ray, clear rigid plastic or glass pane
Various sized brushes and liners
Paint and liners to suit your design and placemats

For monoprinting, paint your image onto a print surface (plastic, a bleached X-ray or glass) and transfer it onto fabric. The print is the reverse of the original. Monoprinting is best suited to bold designs, done quite quickly before the paint dries. I found these ready-made placemats with cheerfully striped borders matching some bright opaque colours I had – just perfect for a children's party-table project. I have always kept my children's early artworks intending to frame or collage them – now I could monoprint them for posterity. Copy your children's artworks onto an X-ray using a brush and opaque fabric paints in the same colours as the originals. If your placemats are light in colour you can use ordinary transparent paints.

1 Place your design under the transparent print surface. Copy onto the print surface using a paintbrush or liner in appropriate colours. To add textural effects, scratch patterns into the wet paint before you print.

2 Turn the print surface over carefully, and place in position on the fabric. Allow to settle before rubbing it gently all over to transfer the print. Lift the print surface off the fabric. Allow fabric to dry thoroughly and heat set.

Hints

Try monoprinted fingerpainting with small children. Paint a wipe-clean surface with a sponge roller. Draw designs into the paint with fingers. Smooth coloured cloth on top, taking care not to shift it while smoothing down. Lift carefully to reveal your monoprinted design. Add variations by pressing hands, leaves, feathers, and stamps into the paint. Or try negative stencils which will leave a blank area where the stencil was.

RIGHT This quilt was a simple quick gift project completed by a large group of friends and family for a couple celebrating their 25th Wedding Anniversary and joint 50th birthday. We all enjoyed drawing and printing our own personalized square for Clara and Anthony. For those who were not able to attend the celebrations or send a gift across continents it was the ideal solution: they sent their A4 sized drawings by fax! The simple line designs were transferred from paper to cloth using the monoprinting method – and in monotone. White lines on different coloured blue and green squares look very effective with the busy colours of the sashing strips. The whole effect is fresh and the theme suitably nautical for the Klitsies' holiday home at Kromme River.

BELOW I found a wonderful collection of fish which had beached themselves during a cold spell. I took them home and traced around the shapes on cut halves of potatoes to use as stamps. These were applied with opaque pearl paint onto black velvet. I used pearl liners to add details to the fish and wavy lines simulating shiny stitching.

Above The poem *In Flanders Fields* by Major John McCrae inspired me on Poppy Day a few years ago to paint this cloth. The background was dry brushed in one direction. When this was dry, I taped diagonally across the cloth, creating diamonds which were dry brushed a little darker. In the lighter diamonds I monoprinted red poppies, facing different ways, using a brush on the plastic. Detail was added to the printed poppies with liner. I copied out the poem in my handwriting – in one direction with a lighter colour on the light diamonds and with a slightly darker colour in the other direction on the darker diamonds.

Below This picture was printed on textured cloth. Using a sponge, I slopped three different brown and beige shades onto the cloth together, creating an almost marbled effect. The nude was monoprinted in layers. Using a drawing from college days, I placed a piece of plastic over it and drew the outline with a brush and light beige. I repeated this a few times, each time using a darker colour in the brown range and a slightly narrower brush. Finally, I added a very thin black line made with a metal-tip liner. I finished off by adding some brown shading around the body.

Left I love making and covering books as gifts for special friends. I decorate the textured fabric covers with paints and dyes in subtle sand colours. I mix sea-sand, sea-weed, fabric paint and glue and apply them to the cover for finishing touches. The cold glue dries transparent with the paint and forms a strong seal on the outside. The sea weed on this book cover was treated in this way to preserve its colour and delicate shape. The otter foot prints were stamped onto the cover using clear opaque base on a foam stamp exactly the size of the Cape clawless otter prints I found while walking on the beach. When the prints dried the opaque base was left raised with chalky relief. This was shaded with transparent brown paint to give depth to the illusion that an otter had just passed by...

stamp & print gallery

Right These musical angels are just the thing to sing you to sleep! They were first traced with a new black pen (the point was finer), and then shaded in. To keep the colours light and fresh this shading was done over a layer of wet extender. The background was clouded with midnight blue over a very pale shade of the same colour. While the background was still wet, stars of various sizes were shadow painted around the edges, using midnight blue. Small stars were also stamped off, creating a different texture.

I cut two stars in two different sizes from foam and used these to stamp on the darker blue stars, when the background was dry, and used a stencil to add the small silver stars that are scattered around. Finally, glitter liner was added here and there for that extra sparkle.

Left Quite different from the mono-printed placemats, this monoprint was done entirely with transparent paint. Masking tape was used to create neat, hard-edged stripes, which were sponged in with peach, blue and green. As these are all light colours, I was able to use transparent paint for the flower, as well. In order that the strelitzias were printed within the boundaries of one wide colour-band at a time, I used paper to mask out any overlapping areas in the adjacent narrow stripes. The flowers are therefore all cut off in some way, enhancing the banded effect.

liquid painting

Liquid painting refers to using watered-down paint and pigment dyes (sun paint). Silk paint may be substituted where we refer to pigment dyes. For ease of reference we also included discharge dyeing or bleaching under liquid painting, although it entails the removal of colour rather than adding colour.

Fabric paint on wet fabric is a really easy technique which relies on the fact that the paint will bleed. It is best for bold, free designs, as it produces a soft and lively effect. Water, flowers, fruit and landscapes are suitable subjects and it is also great for backgrounds. Details can be added when the background is dry. Use bright colours as they dry a lot lighter (unless you want a soft, pale effect). The same colours can be used to add details.

Coarse sea salt or dishwasher salt can be sprinkled onto wet, painted fabric. Salt draws the moisture in different directions, creating an interesting speckled effect. Table salt gives a fine, grained texture to wet, painted cloths. Scatter this through a sieve so that it does not clump together. This technique is especially effective to create a textured background for sea scapes and landscapes and also with sun bleaching.

When the fabric is dry the salt can be shaken off and the cloth washed to remove all traces of salt as it will bind with paint and cause fading. When dry the cloth may be painted on and outlined.

Poured landscape

Were you one of those kids who loved to lie on their backs and look at the sky to see what pictures they could make while watching the clouds float by? Then this one's for you ... This project almost painted itself. It was such fun and went so quickly that I ended up doing several variations with family members all wanting to add something.

You will need

Fabric
Paint: transparent magenta. orange, purple, turquoise, dark charcoal
Liner: dark charcoal

1 Dilute all your colours at least three parts water to one part paint before you start working. Use harmonious colours that blend into one another otherwise you could end up with a muddy finish.

2 Wet your fabric and smooth it onto a board, or spray or sponge wet while stretched. Prop the board up and pour the paint down your fabric. Rest the board on plastic – this is messy!

3 Turn the board around and watch the colours run into one another.

4 Leave flat to dry. The colours dry considerably lighter.

5 Now the fun part: look at the result and try to find shapes and forms to work with. If you can't, turn the fabric around and look at it from different angles and see what you can find. Keep looking and when you find an interesting picture, add some detail with paint and liner and soon you will have a new picture for your wall that almost painted itself! I turned the happy accident of an air bubble, halfway across the fabric into the sun by shading round it. The silhouette was added with dark charcoal, finished with liner (see page 153 for sihouette).

Hint

Seive the diluted paint through a stocking before pouring to get rid of any lumps.

Painting on wet fabric

This is essentially a quick method, but do allow for periods of drying in between the different stages. As the light cloth that I had on my tea table for class had become very stained, I needed a new one where the stains would blend in. When I had almost finished this cloth I felt that it needed a little depth, hence all the liner. As you cannot use a disappearing pen, draw the design in pencil or paint freehand.

You will need

Fabric for a round table cloth
Design enlarged to size (see page 150)
Paintbrushes
Liner
Paint: transparent golden yellow, bright orange, apricot, magenta, purple, dark periwinkle blue, light periwinkle blue
Extender
Liner: transparent navy

SHARE A SECRET

If you're a little slow, or it is really hot and your cloth starts to dry, use a spray bottle to keep the fabric wet.

1 Wet the fabric and wring out so that it is wet, but not dripping. Smooth out on painting surface. The more wrinkled your cloth is the more textured your painting will be. Practice will tell you just how wet. You keep more control when the fabric is drier.

2 Leaving enough space for the border, paint the largest shapes first (pink and purple flowers). You will not have enough space for the larger flowers if you do this the other way round. Vary the shapes you use: round, oval, star, and so on. You don't need to be too careful, as lighter and darker streaks of paint will add to the effect.

3 Fill in with the other flower shapes, ending with the smallest, in this case the orange and yellow.

4 While the cloth is still wet, paint in the blue background. You don't need to go right up to the flower shapes, as the paint bleeding will fill in the gaps for you.

5 Paint the border in rough stripes (see photograph of finished cloth) and leave to dry.

6 Using the same colours you used to make the basic shapes, add in details. Just use brushstrokes to do this.

Straight strokes in the stars, rounded in the round shapes to form roses (well, sort of!), and so on.

7 With a dark blue liner, add details to the flowers and draw leaves here and there around the flowers. You can also use the liner to scribble between the flowers and leaves. If the thought of all this liner fills you with horror, leave it out – the scribbling part at least – but you won't achieve the same textural effect without it.

8 Leave to dry, then fill in In the area around the leaves and flowers with a darker blue, and add darker stripes to the border.

9 Leave to dry thoroughly, heat set and machine hem the table cloth.

LIQUID PAINT ON DRY OR WET FABRIC

- Work on dry fabric with very watery paints. Dilute the paint with 50% warm water, mixing thoroughly. Sieve out lumps. Paint in large flat areas of colour. When painting more than one colour, leave a small gap between areas, allowing the paint to bleed. Here again, bold designs are more suitable and definition can be added with a liner.
- Use a spray bottle, filled with watered down paint, to create sprayed backgrounds. This is crude, but effective for larger cloths – watch out for the drips, or let the drips add to the effect!
- To create cloudy effects with this technique, drop water onto a wet painted cloth and watch the clouds appear (see sarong, page 138).

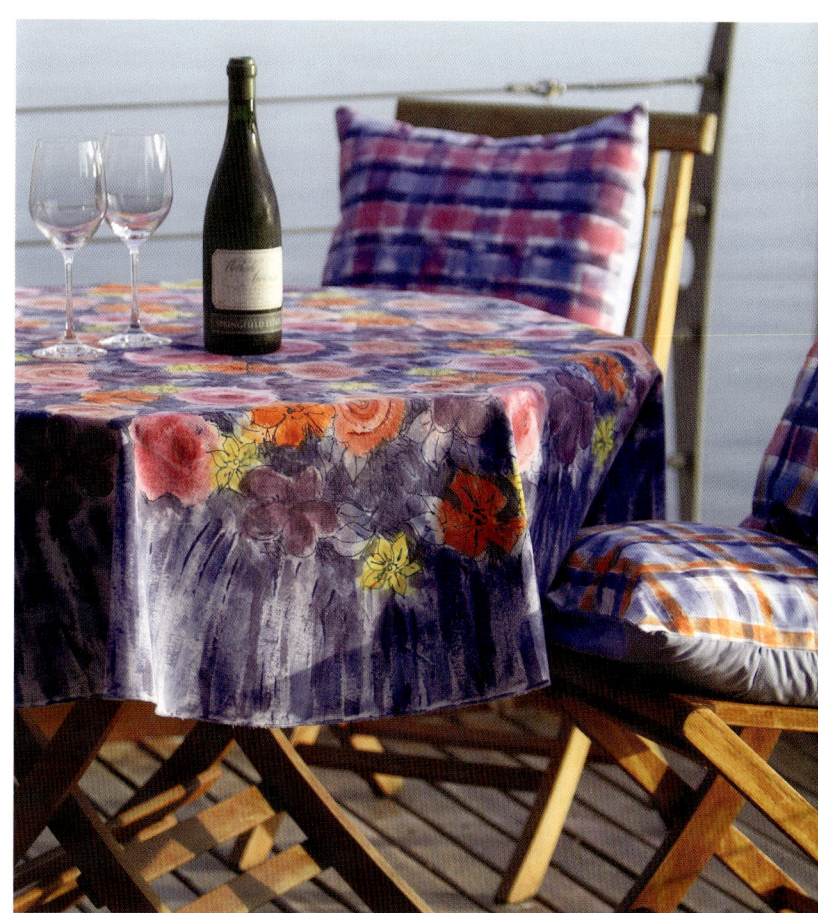

Tie-dye T-shirt

Sun-paint does not develop colour in shaded areas, so the dye will not penetrate to the back of the shirt when you do the front. You will have repeat the process for the back. If you prefer the back of the T-shirt plain, protect the shirt by inserting a plastic bag or plastic covered T-shirt board before you start and just paint the dye on the back afterwards (again, separate the front and back of the shirt with plastic).

You will need

A pre-washed, dry T-shirt
Elastic bands (optional)
Spray bottle with clean water
Protective gloves
Sun paint (liquid dye) in colour of choice, preferably in plastic bottle with nozzle

1 Place clean, dry shirt front-side up on a flat protected surface. Tie-dye the edges of the sleeves by gathering them with elastic bands before you begin (optional).

2 Pinch fingers or press a stick, pencil or tweezers upright into the centre of the T-shirt front and spiral and twist the shirt carefully, keeping the fabric folds flat to get a neat spiral shape.

3 Spray the shirt with clean water from a spray bottle – or fine mister from your garden hose attachment. Do this very gently so that you do not disarrange the twisted folds.

4 Paint, pour or spray sun-paint onto the wet shirt. Wear protective gear as this can be a very messy business. Pouring dye from nozzled bottles is the safest bet.

5 Try pouring patterns, harmonious colour mixes or different strengths of a plain colour as I did for the turquoise T-shirt.

6 Leave the shirt to dry completely, remove any elastic bands, and shake open to reveal your spiral twist.

7 Re-twist and over-dye if you are not satisfied with your first attempt.

SUN BLEACHING WITH BLOCK-OUTS

Sun bleaching produces an almost photographic negative stencil effect on fabric. This technique works best with sun paint. Similar, although more faded, effects can be achieved using watered-down fabric paint.

- Place the fabric onto a board or plastic sheet and paint or sponge the colour onto your fabric.
- Place the wet fabric in the sun with negative stencils, leaves, feathers, shells – anything that will block out the sun – arranged on the painted area. Cut shapes from black garbage bags for the best adherence and light resistance (the takkies were dyed with tiny dolphin stencils, shells and salt on them). If you use leaves, weigh them down with small stones, if necessary. If they do not want to lie flat, sandwich them between layers of kitchen paper towel and iron them flat – this beats pressing them in the phone book for days!
- Leave in the sun until dry and remove block-outs from the cloth. The areas under the stencils will be lighter than the sun-exposed areas.
- Leave blocked-out areas plain, or paint in further details.
- You can create another effect with sun bleaching by painting the entire piece of fabric, crumpling it and leaving it in the sun to dry. As the fabric receives light at different angles, areas shielded from direct sun will be lighter and those more exposed, darker. Creasing and pleating the fabric deliberately will also produce interesting patterns. Lie fabric on grass and it, too, will leave distinctive and interesting textural markings.

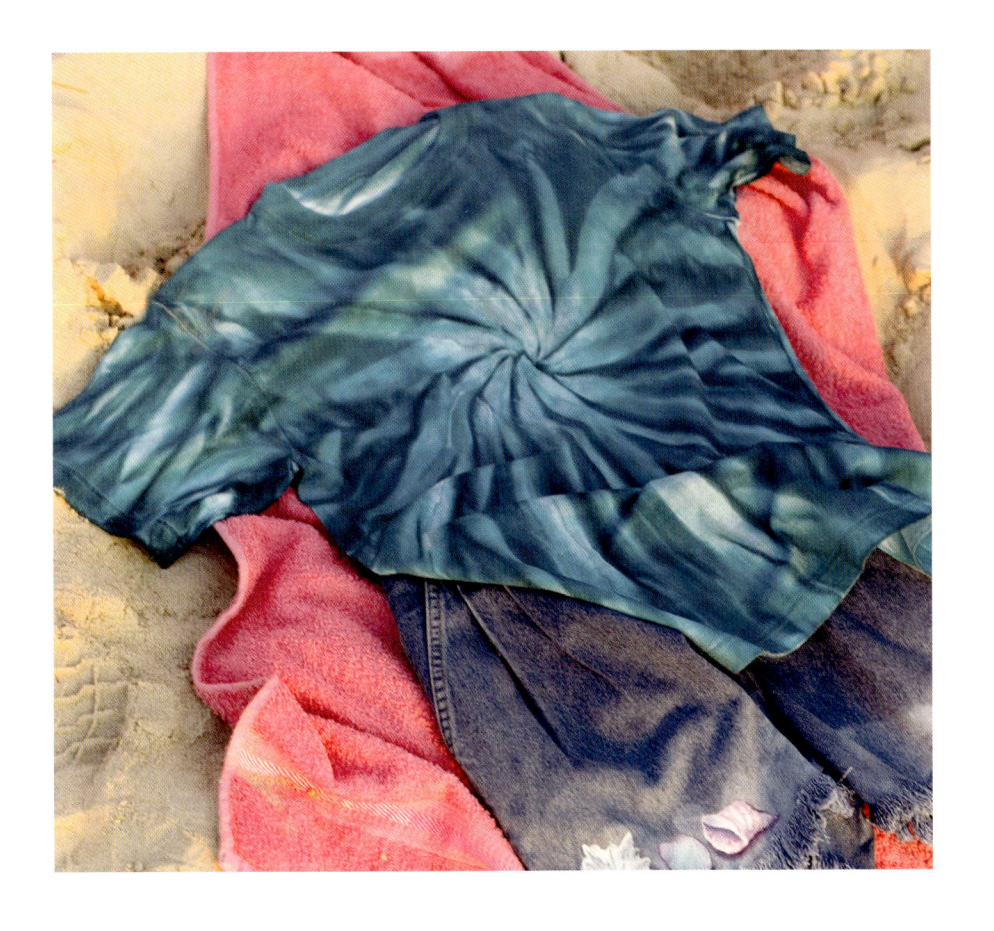

techniques

Sun-painted sarong

You will need

Design enlarged to size (see page 156)
Black plastic bag
Craft knife
Light-weight cotton fabric, 1 m x 1,5 m
Protective gloves
Sun paint (liquid dye) in purple, blue and turquoise, preferably in plastic bottle with nozzle
Paintbrushes
Sponges
Coarse dishwasher salt
Watered-down fabric paint to shade dolphins

Using salt with block-out stencils produces yet another effect. Once again the shadow images can be left at that, or painted and shaded as I did with this sarong.

1 Cut negative dolphin stencils from black plastic garbage bags

2 Wet cotton fabric and pour, sponge or brush turquoise, blue and violet sun-paints across the length of the cloth.

3 Smooth the black stencils onto the fabric along the bottom edge.

4 Sprinkle coarse dishwasher salt across the middle of the sarong just above the dolphin stencils. Then flick more clean water over the sarong and crumple a little around the edges to create extra textural shadows.

5 Leave in the bright sunshine to expose and dry.

6 Remove all stencils and salt and heat set the sarong before washing it to remove the salt residue (some of the paint will wash out with the salt).

7 Paint the dolphins into the block-out shapes using slightly watered down fabric paint. Heat set again so your dolphins won't lose their shading.

Poured sun-paints

Pigment dyes are sometimes marketed as sun-paints. You can also buy liquid-dye base from some suppliers to which you add your own pigments. This liquid dye is strongly colour-fast and hardly requires heat setting. I've yet to discover an effective solvent for it and reserve very old stained clothes for working with it. Watered down fabric paint works well too – mix four parts warm water slowly with one part paint and stir well to dissolve. The technique is dependent on weather – hot sunshine and no wind are essential for success (and we live in Cape Town and Port Elizabeth respectively …)

When I bleached the mildew from my tatty old canvas chair cover, it separated into two pieces – they had been laminated for strength but are perfectly usable separately. I painted one with checks for picnicking and the other waited around to be used for the beach.

You will need

Canvas
Plastic sheet
Liquid dye in purple, blue and turquoise

1 Wet the fabric and lay it on grass or a sheet of plastic. Pour your dyes onto the wet cloth in stripes. They will run and bleed into each other blending to form other harmonious colours.

2 Allow to dry, iron and use. It's that simple!

discharge dyeing

Wonderful effects can be obtained on dark-coloured fabrics by deliberately removing the dye. You can use commercial dye strippers or ordinary thick or liquid household bleach and swimming pool chlorine.
The fabrics must be natural fibre as it is difficult to find strippers for polycottons and other synthetics. Chlorine bleach does not work at all well on synthetics.

Because bleaching uses chlorides, it is absolutely essential to neutralise the process before the cloth dries, otherwise the dye stripper or bleach will eat the fabric fibres and you will be left eventually with a 'holey' cloth!

Household bleach and pool chlorine can be neutralised with ordinary white vinegar. Commercial strippers come with their own sachets of neutralizer and must be used according to the instructions.

Hint

Take great care when working with these materials. Dye stripping uses strong chemicals which can harm your eyes and skin. Always wear protective clothing and gloves and protect your work surface and floor by covering with newsprint or plastic. Mistakes cannot simply be washed out.

Bleached landscape

We used good quality bleach (some bleaches work better than others) and granular swimming pool chlorine for this cushion cover. You need to work fairly quickly so have all your equipment and ideas sorted out before you start.

1 Protect the area outside your picture with pieces of absorbent cardboard (cut up an old cereal box and use inside up. Don't use plastic as the bleach runs off and can damage the surrounding area – or worse, drip onto your shoes!)

2 Mark off the area to be bleached with torn masking tape – the rough edges bleach interesting lines. Blank out any area you want to keep black (such as mountains), with torn masking tape.

3 Spray bleach solution onto the picture area with a fine mist spray. Within seconds it will start discharging the dye producing a fine grainy tan colour. Depending on the base dye used, the discharge *can* turn the black to green, rust, purple or grey – but usually tan.

4 Add light areas, for example the sun or clouds, by painting them in with neat thick bleach.

5 Sprinkle granular chlorine where you want light textural spotting, for example a starry sky or rough foliage, and sprinkle or spray with a little water to activate the chlorine.

6 Leave until the picture begins to develop and rinse immediately in a bucket of neutraliser.

7 Allow to dry and make your cushion cover.

Hints
- For fun, why not try bleaching old T-shirts and denims – experiment with different colours and see what results you get (see page 20).
- You can have great fun embellishing the bleached design with paints, threads and beads.

You will need

Black cotton
Strong thick household bleach
Granular pool chlorine
Wide masking tape
Cereal box cardboard
Spray bottle filled with 1 part liquid household bleach to 3 parts water
Old bristle and nylon brushes
Bucket of neutraliser (1 cup of vinegar to 4 litres of water)
Materials to make cushion cover

All the items in this picture were sun painted using purple, blue and turquoise. Fern leaves and salt were scattered across the throw to create a simple leafy pattern. Stencils of the fairy, the sun shape and border were used as block outs on the fairy cushion, as well as butterfly confetti. This created lighter areas which were easily painted in later with white opaque and transparent colours, to add details. Fine willow leaves were used in the body of the cushion while the patterned leafy details were painted in with a fine brush and liner. Beware who you paint this fairy for: My god-daughter, on receiving a T-shirt with this fairy on the front refused to wear it, as, said she: "That fairy hasn't got proper wings – it can't fly!" The flowers on the cushion at the back were first starched, and then sun painted when the starch was dry. Detail was added by placing some lacy weeds onto the wet paint.

The fabric for this windbreak was first wet under a tap and wrung out, rather than spraying wet *in situ*. This created a very textured effect, together with the sea salt that was sprinkled over the entire cloth after the stencils were put in position. It was sun painted in wavy stripes, using orange at the top and bottom and then adding stripes of magenta, purple, blue and finally turquoise in the middle. Stencils of the two large fish were placed slightly towards one side with stencils of smaller fish filling in.

When dry, the cloth was shaken out and washed to clear it completely of salt. The two large fish were painted in with transparent paint and the details added with liner. Details of curls and dots were added to the background with a brush, using similar colours to the wavy stripes.

Right These *Dancing Gals* started life as all sorts of colours being poured over a piece of cloth. Their creator, Elsabé Adams, found them amidst the drama and excitement. She saw the shapes and enhanced them by shading quite strongly around them, taking care not to totally shade out the vibrant background. She decorated the wonderful dresses by adding liner in metallic colours and shading into the shapes that she'd made with additional colours.

Below This 'poured' creation, also by Elsabé Adams, could just as easily have been a landscape, if turned on its side. More subdued than the dancing ladies, these cloaked ladies have far less detail, but are just as effective. One can still see the effect of air bubbles underneath the cloth as it was drying, especially on the purple cloak.

Below A close up of the sunpainted sarong with the shaded dolphins clearly shows the dimension and movement achieved by shading and highlighting.

Designs

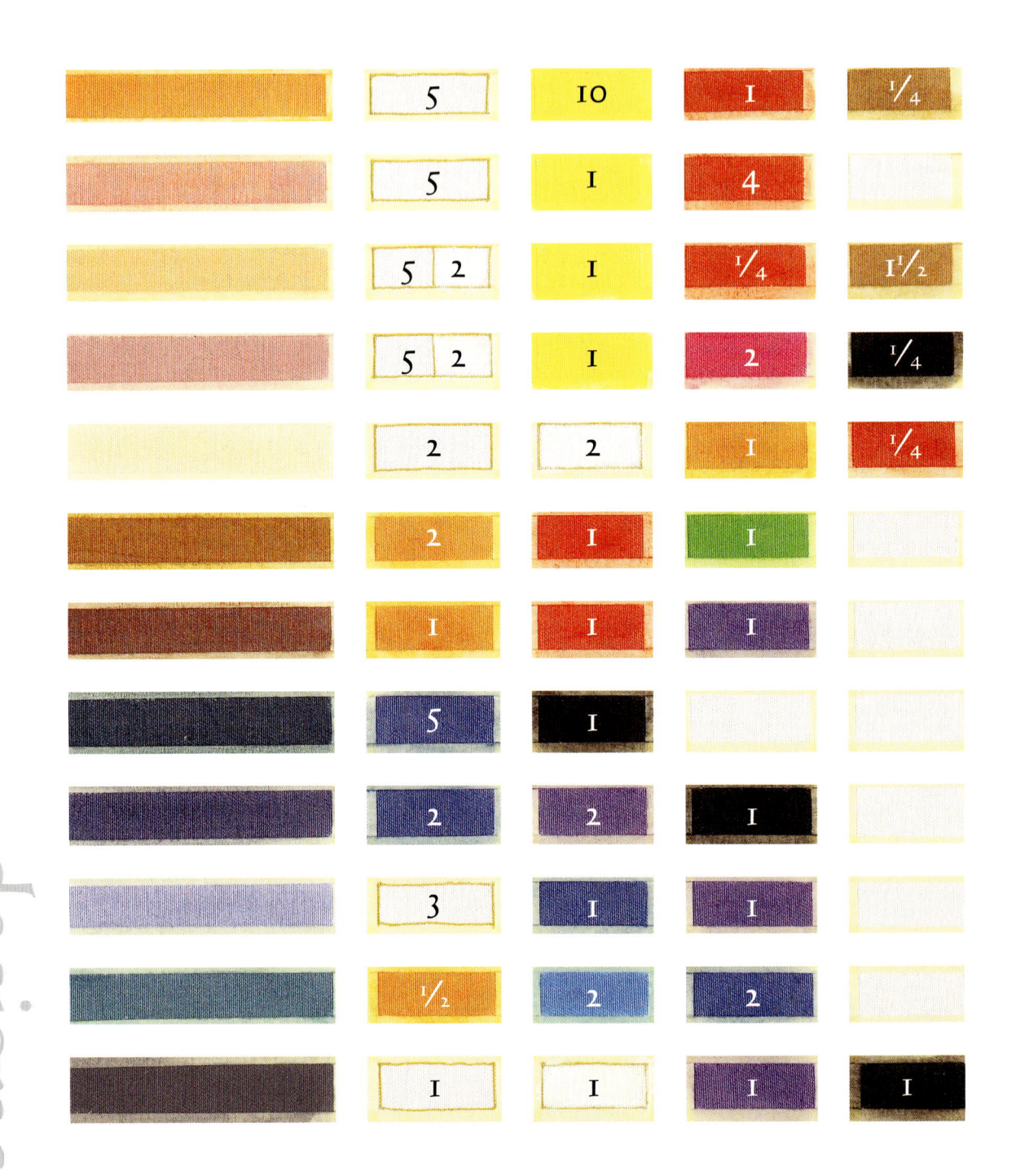

orange	5	10	1	1/4
pink	5	1	4	
pale yellow	5 | 2	1	1/4	1 1/2
dusty pink	5 | 2	1	2	1/4
cream	2	2	1	1/4
brown	2	1	1	
rust	1	1	1	
navy	5	1		
purple	2	2	1	
lavender	3	1	1	
teal	1/2	2	2	
dark	1	1	1	1

144

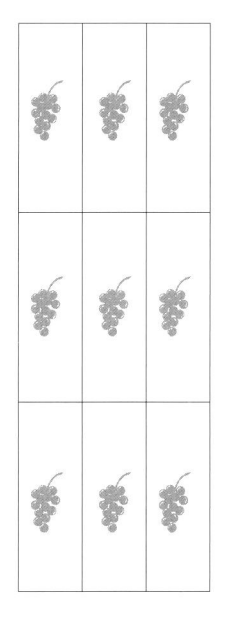

Block repeat

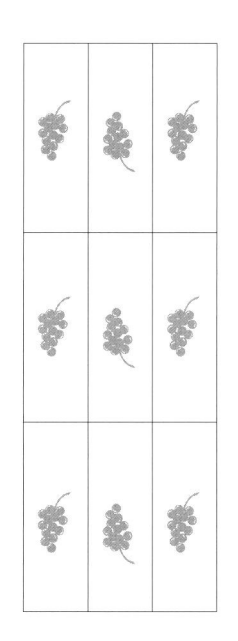

Reverse block repeat

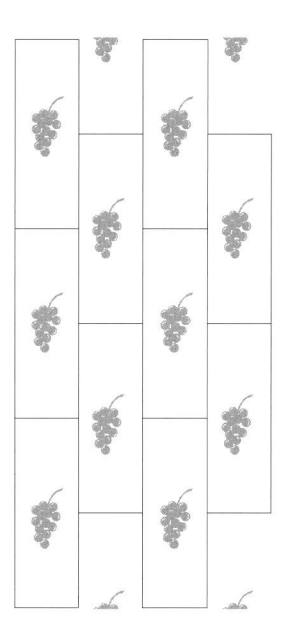

Half-drop repeat

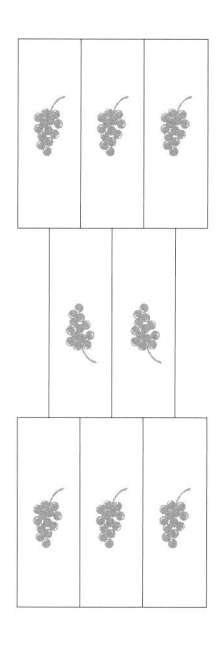

Brick vertical reverse

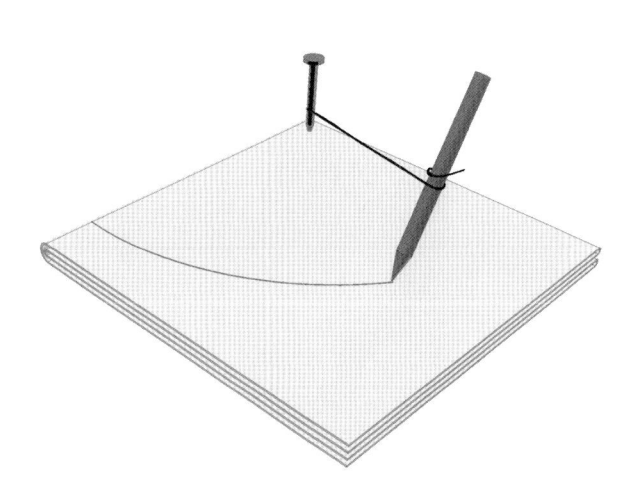

Cutting a circle

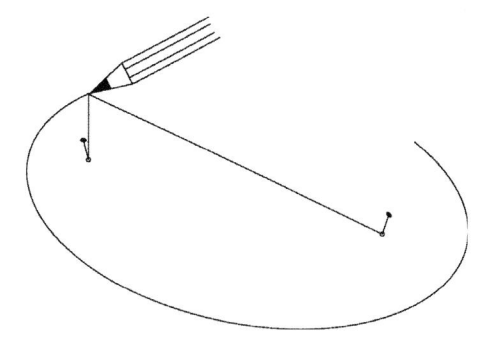

Drawing an oval

African pot

Lizard

designs

146

Cherries

Olives

designs

147

Adinkra symbols

Bese saka (a bunch of cola nuts). Abundance

Nsoramma (star – child of the heavens). We are all God's children

Hye-wo-ho-nhye (he who burns be not burned). Loyalty and forgiveness

Akoko nan tia ne ba a endum no. Teaching with patience, also compassion and protection

Gye Nyame – God almighty all present and knowing. Symbol of the immortality of God

Nyame Dua – God's tree. God is present in all things

Foofoo. Warning against envy

Aya – the fern. Courage

Dwannimmen – ram's horn. Wisdom and humility

Fihankra – the complete house. Security and protection

Gyawu atiko – bravery

Sign of the return: Look at your past and you will recognise your future

Ani bere a ennso gya anka m'ani abere koo: a serious expression is not necessarily a sign of irritation and anger

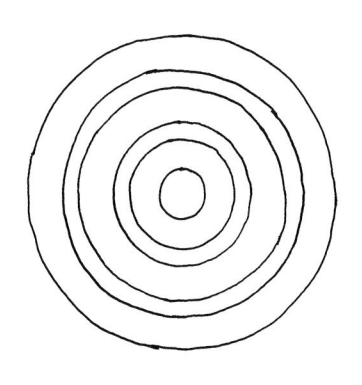

Adinkrahene – king of the adinkra designs. Magnanimity – generosity of spirit

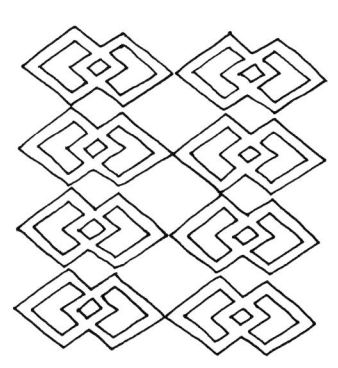

Epa – handcufs. Law stands above the people

Spirals

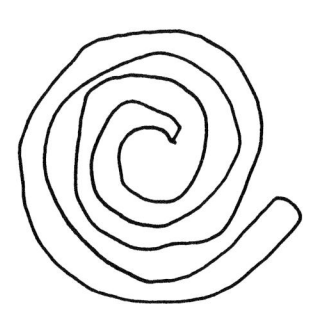

Floral design for wet painting

Spiral design for velvet bag

Strelitzia

designs

Study in textures

Butterfly for lino stamp

designs

152

Poppies combined

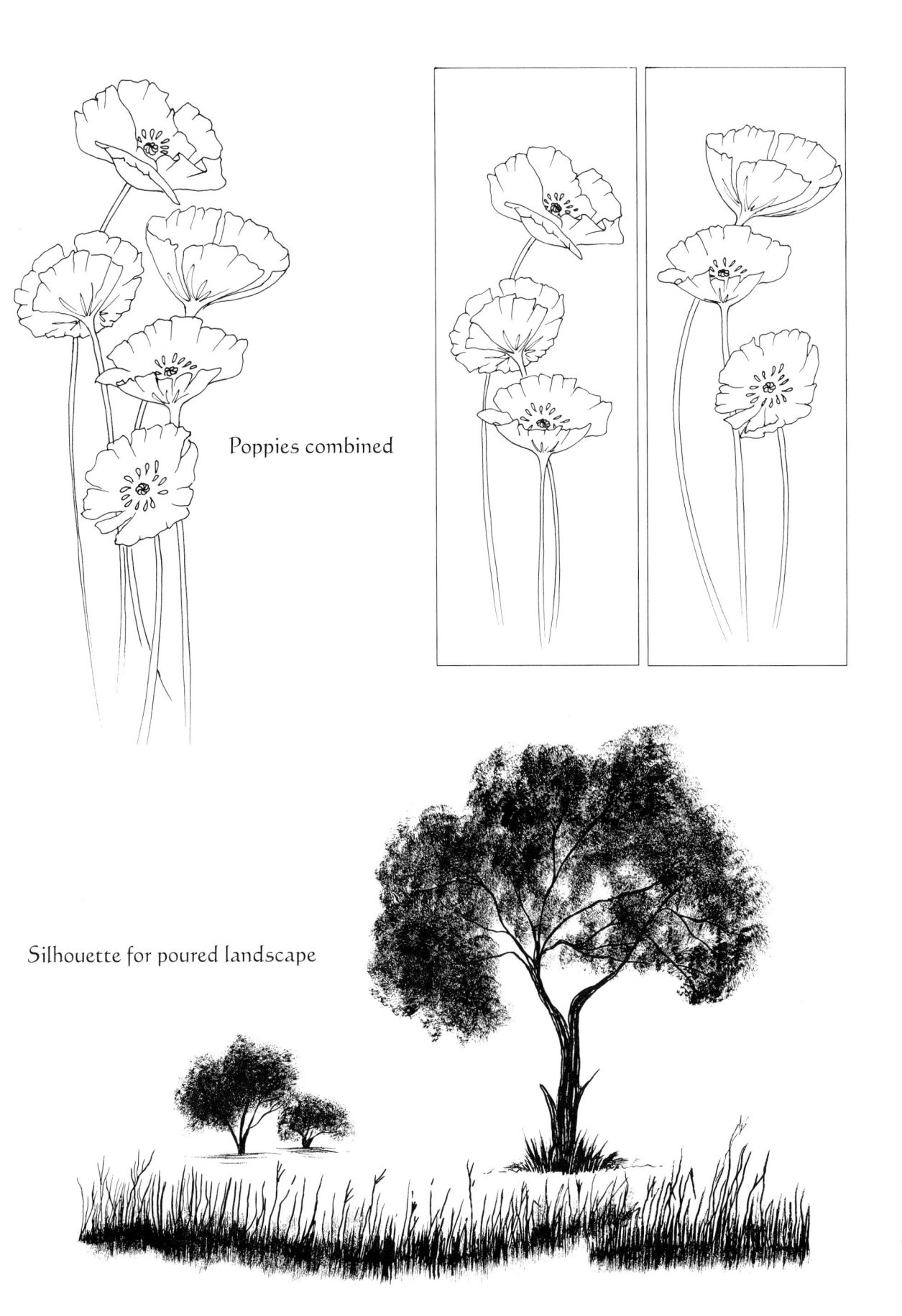

Silhouette for poured landscape

designs

Dolphins

Shaded face

Scraped baskets

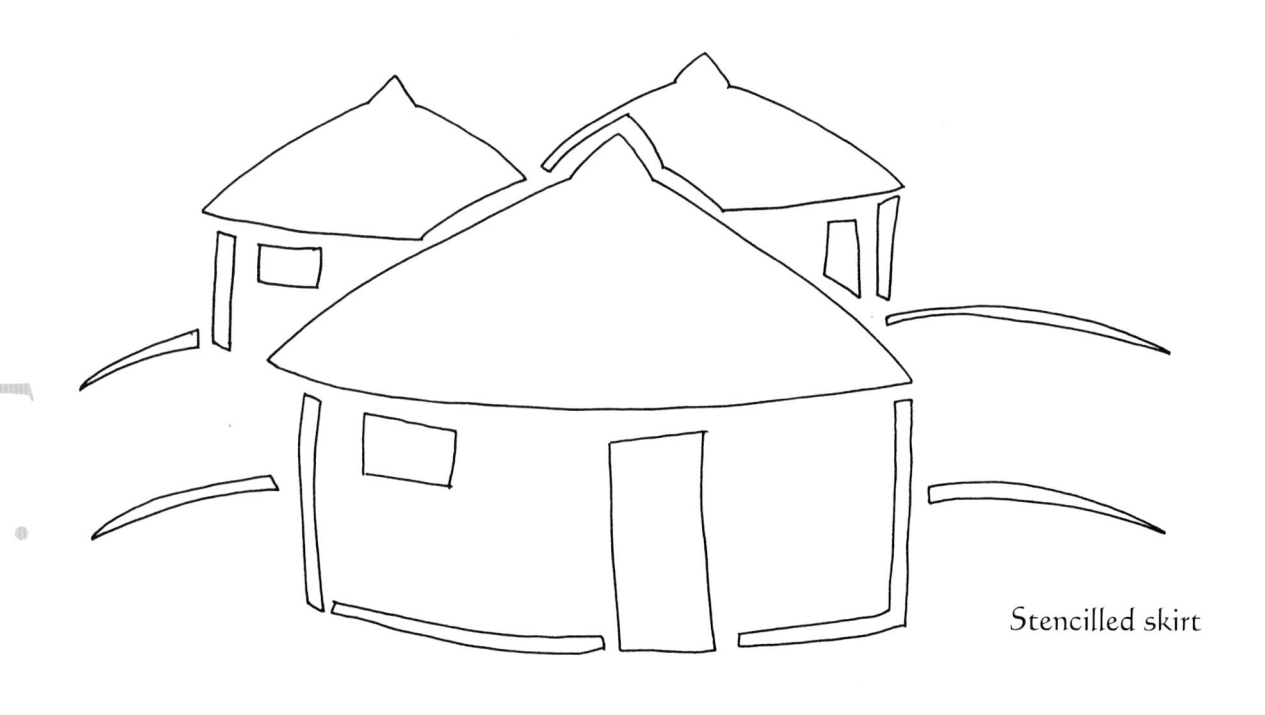

Stencilled skirt

Stencilled skirt

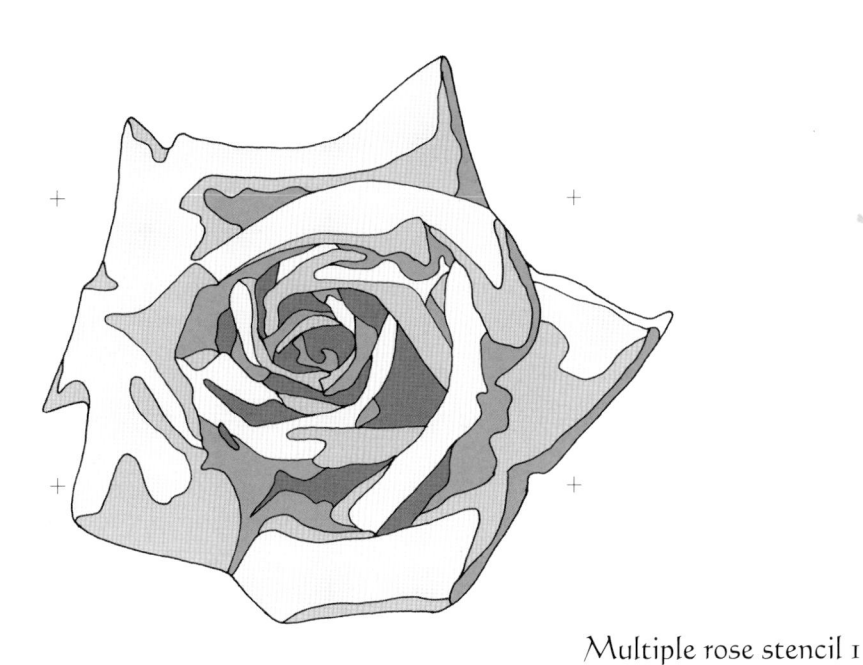

Multiple rose stencil 1

combined

designs

light

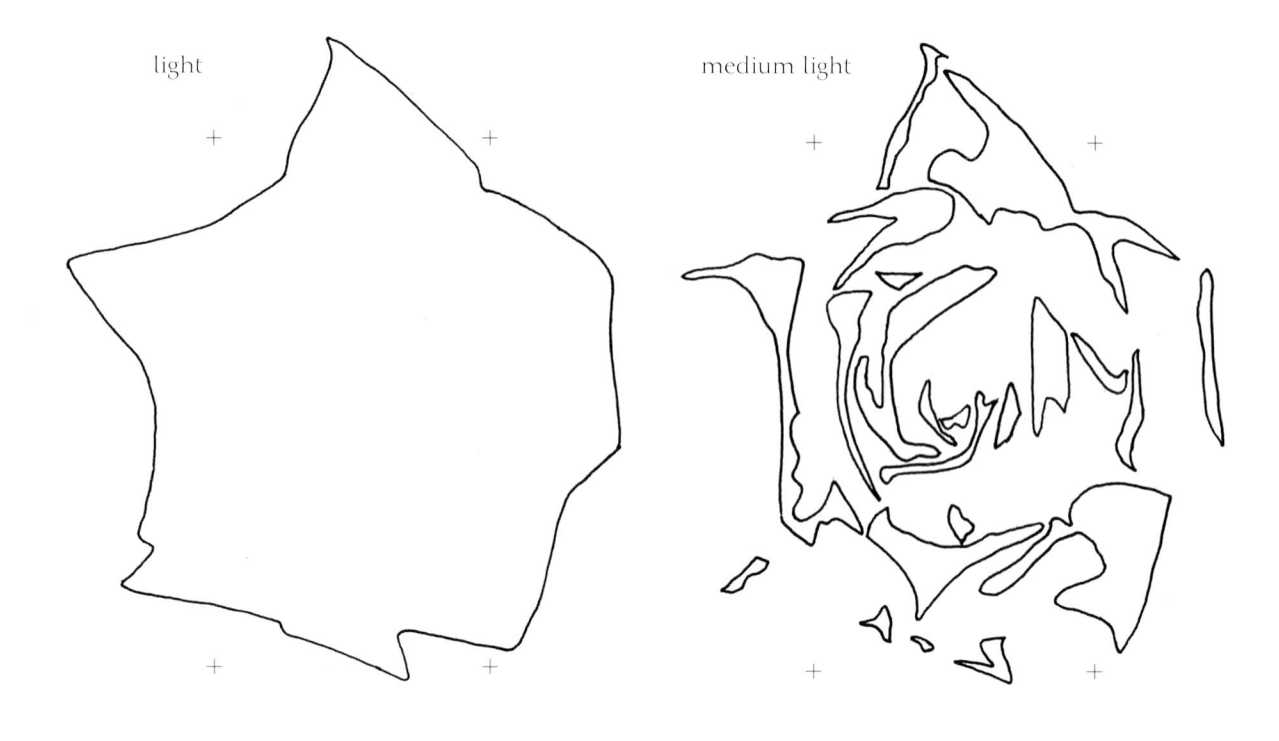

medium light

Leave enough plastic or acetate around each stencil, and ensure that the registration marks align exactly before stencilling

dark

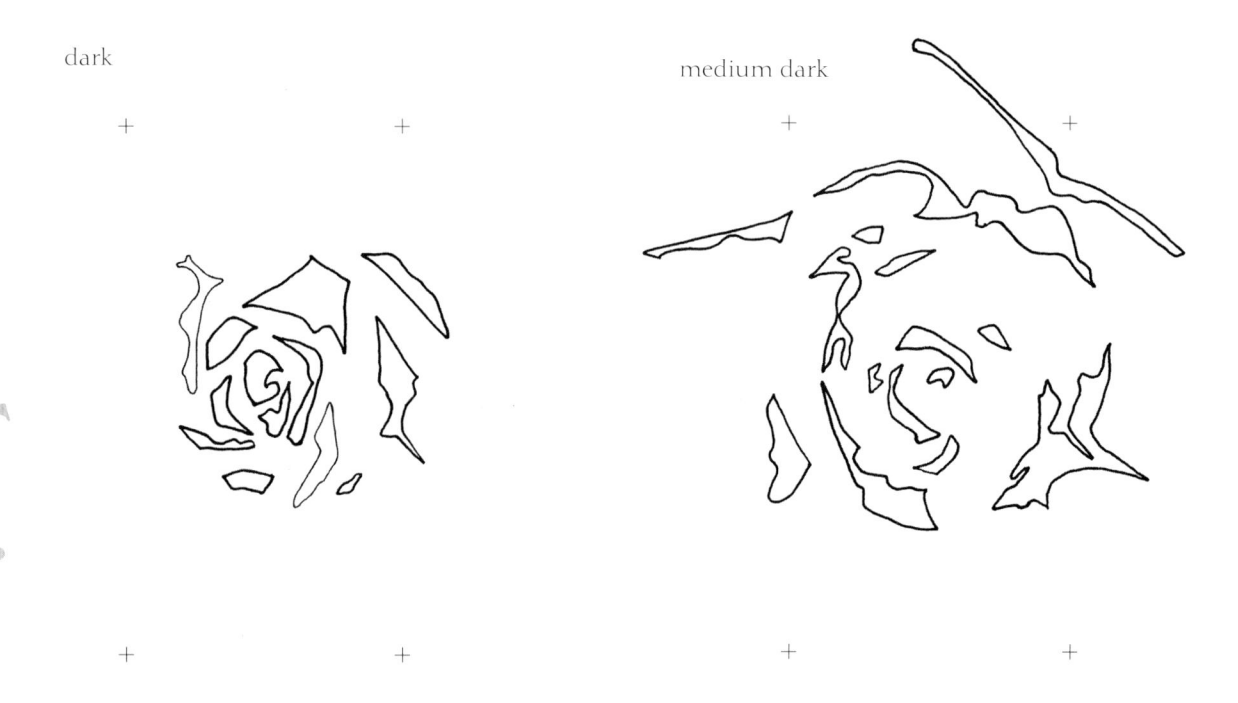

medium dark

Multiple rose stencil 1

+ combined + + dark +

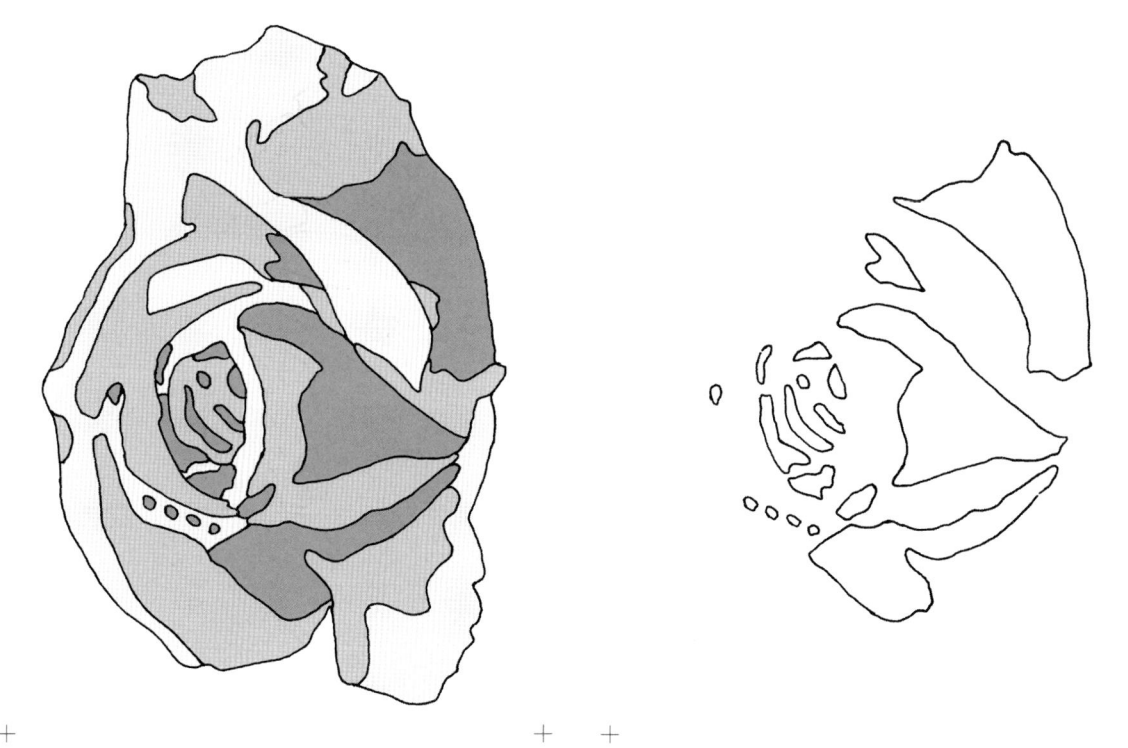

Leave enough plastic or acetate around each stencil, and ensure that the registration marks align exactly before stencilling

+ light + + medium +

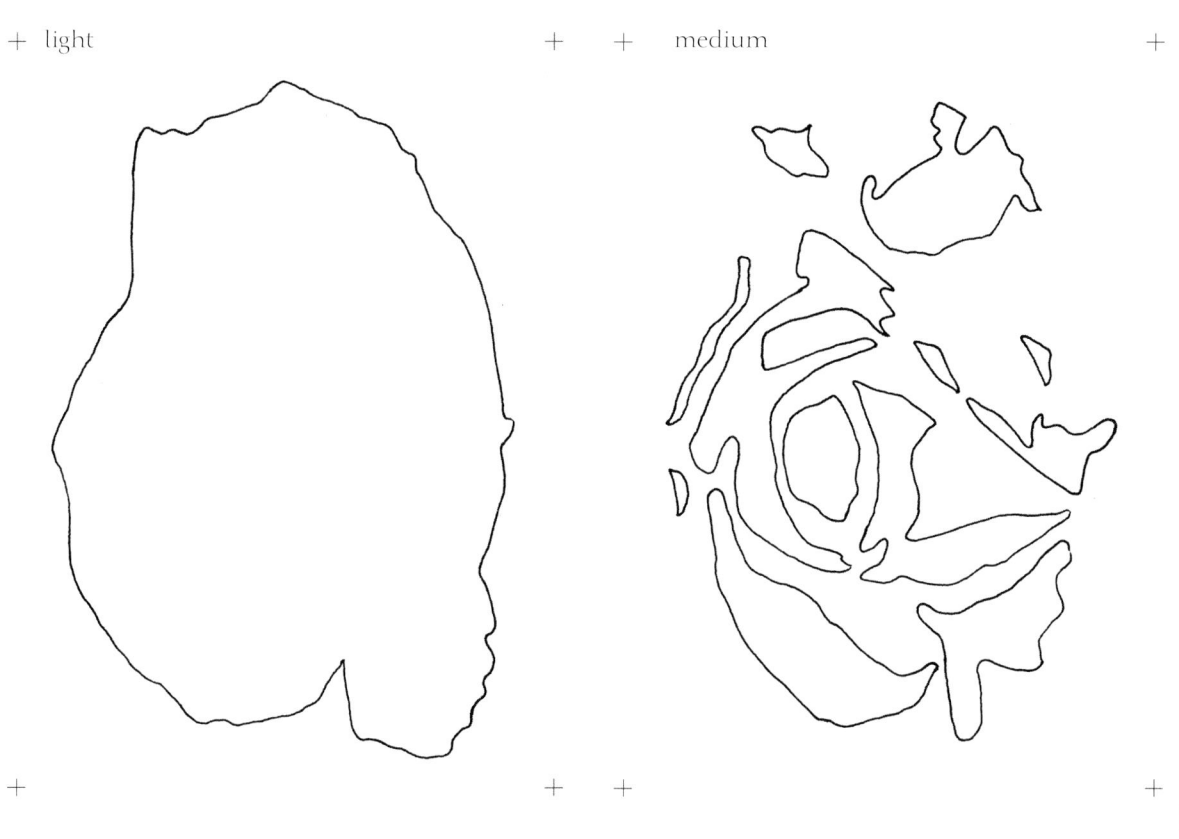

Multiple rose stencil 2

Colour wheel (Angie's wheel)

	A5 210x148cm	A4 297x210cm	A3 297x420cm	A2 420x594cm	A1 594x841cm	A0 841x1189cm
A5	100%	142%	200%	283%	566%	803%
A4	70%	100%	142%	200%	383%	566%
A3	50%	70%	100%	142%	200%	283%
A2	35%	50%	70%	100%	142%	200%
A1	25%	35%	50%	70%	100%	142%
A0	12,5%	17,5%	25%	35%	50%	100%

Standard enlargement percentages